# A LITTLE
# LOWER
## THAN THE
# ANGELS

GOD CREATED YOU AWESOME
AND POWERFUL: HOW TO KEEP YOUR BODY,
SOUL, AND SPIRIT STRONG AND HEALTHY

# GRAEME LOFTUS

DESTINY IMAGE™ EUROPE srl
Via Maiella, 1
66020 San Giovanni Teatino (Ch) - Italy

*"Changing the world, one book at a time."*

This book and all other Destiny Image™ Europe books are available at Christian bookstores and distributors worldwide.

To order products, or for any other correspondence:

DESTINY IMAGE™ EUROPE srl
Via Acquacorrente, 6
65123 - Pescara - Italy
Tel. +39 085 4716623 - Fax +39 085 9431270
E-mail: info@eurodestinyimage.com

Or reach us on the Internet: **www.eurodestinyimage.com**

ISBN: 978-88-89127-95-7

*For Worldwide Distribution, Printed in the U.S.A.*

1 2 3 4 5 6 7 8/13 12 11 10

*May God Himself, the God of peace, sanctify you through and through. May your whole spirit, soul and body be kept blameless at the coming of our Lord Jesus Christ. The One who calls you is faithful and He will do it* (1 Thessalonians 5:23-24).

# DEDICATION

To my two sons, Jeremy and Benjamin, who although they did not intentionally set out to do so, nor were even probably aware that they were involved, have nevertheless focused aspects of my humanity for me. In their own separate and different ways, they have helped me gain a more insightful awareness of these aspects of who Jesus has created me to be. In the challenging and sometimes confronting process of living with them, and in the light of the Gospel, I have grown to affirm my humanity, knowing that the destiny of the journey is revealed in the one true man, Jesus.

# ACKNOWLEDGMENTS

I wish to acknowledge the strong encouragement given me right through the writing of this book from my wife, Janis, together with my step-children, Dimitrios and Vasiliki.

I am also deeply grateful for the spiritual and financial support that has been given to me by the following generous individuals:

- Katrina and Simon Reye
- Karen and Paul Fehlberg
- Angela and Ross Howard
- Nerida and Ian Miller
- Sally and Geoff Crews
- Dr. Ian Wilson.

# TABLE OF CONTENTS

# INTRODUCTION

Before we explore aspects of the human nature that God has created us with, it is helpful to establish principles that will greatly assist us in understanding the issues at hand and form sound biblical parameters. We need the Bible to transform our minds to think like Jesus does about the created form He has given us. Some worldviews are so dominant and prevailing in life today that unless we take time to do this, many preconceived ideas we unconsciously hold concerning terms used will confuse the issues. We are heavily influenced by our cultural background, and when we pick up the Bible as our point of reference in this discussion, it is imperative to understand its cultural patterns of thought in order to use them as a norm.

The Bible, in both the Old and New Testaments, is through and through a Hebrew book. Its culture and thought patterns are all characteristically Hebrew as lived in the times in which it was written. It cannot be properly understood, or appreciated without taking this into consideration. The New Testament, however, even though it continued to embody a Hebrew way of thinking, was written in the Greek language, at a time in history when Greek culture and patterns of thinking saturated and dominated the whole of the then known world. The great Greek philosophers had profoundly impacted society, and have continued to do so down through the ages. The difference between Hebrew thought and Greek thought is enormous. In this twenty-first century we still, consciously or unconsciously, adopt one or the other of these patterns. And whichever we choose has a dramatic impact on the way we think of ourselves and, as a consequence, the way we live and die in the world.

## GREEK THINKING

The ancient Greeks divided everything into two realms—either matter or spirit. For them, everything material, including the human body, was an inferior "shadow" or approximation of a pure ideal existing somewhere in the spirit realm. The spirit realm alone was idealized and sought after. The material realm was thought of as substandard, bad, and even essentially evil. It kept humans apart from the spirit realm and thus became its enemy.[1]

The human body was thought of as a prison of the human spirit and treated accordingly. Some stoical Greeks disciplined the physical aspects of their body in an endeavor to not hamper their inner spirit in its existence. Others perceived their bodies as something that, at best, had only a temporary existence, and treated it for self-indulgent pleasure, believing it to be irrelevant in the long run. They ate, drank, and were merry. They looked forward to the time when the inner spirit would finally be released and liberated at death to merge with a greater, universal, eternal spirit.

This very abstract way of separating everything into two is called dualism and was characteristic of all the dominant Greek philosophers, especially men such as Plato and Socrates. By the time Jesus lived in the first century, this way of thinking had essentially become universal throughout most of the biblical world and it heavily influenced all surrounding nations. It stood in sharp contrast, however, to Hebrew patterns of thought that continued to doggedly and persistently survive in Palestine in the face of other nations and their cultures. Generally speaking, most Jews had stubbornly resisted the encroachment of any foreign culture, including the milieu of Greek thinking that had saturated the Roman world of the day.

## HEBREW THINKING

Hebrew people did not divide their world into two compartments like the Greeks did. Under the influence of the Old Testament, they thought of everything that existed as a unity that was very concrete rather than abstract. God had created everything material in the universe, and according to the Genesis account, it was not only good, but indeed "very good." (See Genesis 1:31.) Genesis chapter 3 describes the tragic account of how humanity alienated itself from God and introduced into the world what the Bible calls "sin."[2] Every aspect of the created order has been markedly impacted by sin. The earth as it now exists is a long way from the pristine state in which it had been created originally. The Creator is not responsible for raping the environment for economic profit, the destruction of the ozone layer, or climate warming with all its disastrous effects. The blight of sickness, death, drought, bushfires, earthquakes, tsunamis, famines, floods, and epidemic diseases has to be laid at the feet of humanity. We are the ones who cut ourselves off from trusting our Creator and now helplessly watch the unravelling of our irresponsible and insane desire for independence from Him.

In recognizing this, however, we must not conclude that matter itself has become intrinsically sinful or bad or evil as the Greeks assumed. All matter is morally neutral. Sin is a human problem that has had a ruinous impact on every good thing given to us by God as a trust.

The difference between the Greek and Hebrew understanding of the body has been classically illustrated by Oscar Cullman as he reflected on the death of Socrates and the death of Jesus.[3] There were remarkable similarities in these two deaths. Both men had their disciples and followers surrounding them at the time. On the one hand, Socrates committed suicide by drinking a glass of hemlock. His disciples were singing because they believed that his spirit was about to be released from its bodily confines into the realm of the wider, everlasting spirit of all things. During the end of Jesus' life on earth, however, "…Jesus cried out in pain and wept in sorrow as He offered up priestly prayers to God. Because He honored God, God answered Him. Though He was God's Son, He learned trusting-obedience by what He suffered…" (Heb. 5:7 TM).

## ENDNOTES

1.  George Eldon Ladd, *The Pattern of New Testament Truth* (Grand Rapids, MI: Eerdmans Publishing Co., 1968), 13-40.

2.  See Romans 5:21.

3.  Oscar Cullmann, *Immortality of the Soul or Resurrection of the Dead?* (London: Epworth Press, 1958), 19-27.

# CHAPTER ONE

# THE HUMANITY
# OF JESUS

# THE HUMANITY
# OF JESUS

As a Hebrew, Jesus believed that apart from a bodily resurrection, His very existence was terminated (see Mark 15:34; Job 14:14-15; Rev. 20:6). In His divine nature, He chose a human body in which to reveal His Father's heart to the world. Jesus, however, was not part man and part God. He was fully man and fully God. He was just as much a man as if He had never been God. If He was deprived of sleep and food, He became tired and hungry. When crucified on the cross, His blood was authentic human blood.

At the same time, however, Jesus was just as much God as if He had never been man as evidenced in the way He received worship and forgave sins. He was the unique God-man.

When Jesus was resurrected, He went out of His way to show the disciples that He was not a ghost and still had a corporeal body (see Luke 24:36-46). He called them to touch His risen body and ate food in their presence. Jesus has bound Himself to humanity with a tie that will never be broken for the ages of eternity (see Heb. 7:24). At His second coming, every Christian will receive a body like His glorified corporeal body (see Phil. 3:20-21; 1 Cor. 15:35-44).

It was His teaching of the resurrection of the body that formed such a great stumbling block for most Greek-thinking people. Why should they look forward to a bodily resurrection, when they had spent their whole life seeking to minimize or escape from its impact on their life in this world and their ultimate existence? The Greeks at Athens listened patiently to Paul preaching to them on Mars Hill, but mocked him and walked away when he endeavored to emphasize the significance of Christ's resurrection. It was foolishness to them (see Acts 17:32; 1 Cor. 1:18–2:5).

The early church subsequently experienced a number of heresies centered on variations of Greek thinking that forced Christian leaders to clarify the nature of Jesus' humanity. Foremost among these were schools of thought that have become known as Docetism and Adoptionism. Docetism comes from the Greek word *dokeō* ("to seem"). It is the belief that Jesus' physical body was an illusion, as was His crucifixion. Jesus, they maintained, only seemed to have a physical body and seemed to physically die, but in reality He was incorporeal, a pure spirit, and hence could not physically die.[1] Docetism was condemned by church leaders at the Council of Chalcedon in A.D. 451.

Adoptionism is a belief that Jesus was born merely human and that He became divine later in His life. By these accounts, Jesus earned the title Christ through His sinless devotion to the will of God, thereby becoming the perfect sacrifice to redeem humanity. Adoptionism believes that the two key points in Jesus' life were His baptism and His resurrection that led to the Father adopting Him as Christ, the Messiah. At His baptism, Adoptionists believe that God gave Jesus His miraculous power and divine authority after He had proved His holiness. This belief arose among early Christians seeking to reconcile the claims that Jesus was the Son of God with the radical monotheistic belief of Judaism that God did not exist in more than one personhood. Eventually, it too was rejected by the First Council of Nicaea in A.D. 325.

So pervasive was Greek culture and Greek thinking during biblical times that not all Jews were impervious to its impact. There is an incident recorded in the life of the early church that highlights this reality. Not long after its beginnings, a situation arose where "…Grecian Jews among them complained against the Hebraic Jews because their widows were being overlooked in the daily distribution of food" (Acts 6:1).

The apostle Paul had to constantly counteract the faulty influence of this Grecian cultural worldview wherever he went in the non-Jewish Gentile world. Nowhere is this clearer than his letters to the church in Corinth, a city in Greece. It becomes obvious, for example, that many of the members there had rejected his teaching on the resurrection of Christ because of the heritage of their Greek understanding of death (see 1 Cor. 15:12). He spends a lengthy chapter in First Corinthians 15 addressing this issue to correct their misunderstanding. It seems also that some married couples were refraining from normal marital relations for the same reason. They drew heavily on Jesus' teaching that in the resurrection men and women are "...beyond marriage. As with the angels, all our ecstasies and intimacies then will be with God" (Matt. 22:30 TM). This became their measure of life in the spiritual realm. From their perspective, any marital engagement of the body was influencing their spiritual life in a negative way, and so they chose to not actively engage with each other sexually (see 1 Cor. 7:1-5). It is generally thought that this was also the basis upon which some women began to remove any covering of their heads during worship (see 1 Cor. 11:6). To them it was a statement concerning the "unspiritual" distinction between men and women that did not exist in the realm of spirit. This focus on super-spirituality is evident also in the issue of tongue-speaking that Paul addresses in chapters 12-14. The Corinthian believers were seeking to speak in the language of angels (see 1 Cor. 13:1) as an evidence of their connection with the higher "spirit" world and thus imply a spiritual maturity and superiority over those who could not speak in tongues. Paul spoke against this faulty pattern of Greek thinking and had to clarify that love, the fruit of the Holy Spirit, was more important in God's eyes than any gift of the Holy Spirit which did not edify the whole community (see 1 Cor. 13:1-10; 14:1-5).

## EARLY CHRISTIANITY

As Christianity entered the second and third centuries, history reveals that this pattern of Greek thinking came to dominate the church in all aspects of theology and practice. Instead of engaging in the corrupt world, many Christians sought spiritual solace in the desert. Some became virtual hermits. Simon Stylites (ca. A.D. 390-459), for example, who had been strongly influenced by the Byzantine church of his day, sat on top of a pole situated 25 miles west of Aleppo in Syria for 37 years. As the medieval church developed, many men and women sought a similar lifestyle in the isolation of a monastery and, believing this to be the only way to develop their human spirit, dedicated their life to celibacy and chastity. The epitome of spiritual virtue became the "virgin" Mary.

## AN EMERGING REDISCOVERY OF OUR
## GOD-CREATED HUMAN NATURE

It was not until the twentieth century, however, that Hebrew patterns of thinking were rediscovered by several biblical scholars and have continued to reshape biblical studies and our understanding of humanity from God's perspective. Hans Kung, a well-known Swiss Roman Catholic theologian, in his book *Eternal Life?*, gives some interesting insight into these subjects. On pages 140-143 he writes,

> In the "eternal punishment" (Matt. 25:46) of the Last Judgment the stress lies on the fact that this punishment is definitive, final, decisive for all eternity, but not on the eternal duration of the torment. Neither in Judaism nor in the New Testament is there any uniform view of the period of punishment for sin. In addition to statements about eternal punishment, there are texts which assume a complete destruction ("eternal corruption," 2 Thess. 1:9). And throughout Church history, in addition to the traditional dualism, the possibility of annihilation ... (has) been defended.[2]

Lutheran theologian, Oscar Cullmann, has been even more definite in his defense of Hebrew thinking in his monumental work, *Immortality of the Soul or Resurrection of the Dead?* With a great deal of insight he says in Chapter 2,

Behind the corporeal appearance Plato senses the incorporeal, transcendent, pure Idea. Behind the corrupted creation,
under sentence of death, the Christian sees the future creation brought into being by the resurrection, just as God
willed it. The contrast, for the Christian, is not between the
body and the soul, not between outward form and Idea, but
rather between the creation delivered over to death by sin
and new creation; between the corruptible, fleshly body and
the incorruptible resurrection body.[3]

Having said all this, let us consider First Thessalonians 5:23-24 as
a starting point for a reflection on human nature.

*May God himself, the God of peace, sanctify you through and*
*through. May your whole spirit, soul and body be kept blame-*
*less at the coming of our Lord Jesus Christ. The one who calls*
*you is faithful and he will do it.*

God is here described as the God of "peace," the Greek equivalent to the Hebrew word, *shalom*. This is not primarily defining any
peaceful inner emotion, but rather the quality of life experienced in
the Kingdom of God. Paul is asking that the God who offers us this
type of life desires us to let Him sanctify us, make us thoroughly
holy. We are to set ourselves apart totally to Him so that our whole
being may be blameless when Jesus returns climactically at the end
of time as we now experience it.

It is important to notice that Paul doesn't urge us to attain sinlessness in all aspects of our humanity before that moment. To be blameless is to have entered into a saving relationship with Jesus. From that
time onward, God does not blame us for the reality of sin that, although remaining in our human nature, no longer controls us. It is
only at the return of Jesus that this "corruptible" puts on incorruption
(see 1 Cor. 15:51-54). We who have the firstfruits of the Holy Spirit still
groan within ourselves because of residual sin until the redemption of
our bodies at the resurrection (see Rom. 8:22-23; Phil. 3:20-21). Our
sins have been forgiven through the atonement of Jesus and if we claim
that provision—trusting its reality—it gives us a foretaste of shalom.
"For God so loved the world that He gave His one and only Son, that

whoever believes in him shall not perish but *have* eternal life" (John 3:16). Eternal life, here, is more than life that lasts for eternity. It is, rather, the quality of life described by the term *shalom*. If we have maintained a saving relationship with God "at the coming of our Lord Jesus Christ," then we will be with Him for the rest of eternity.

In a very valid sense, the expression, "your whole spirit, soul and body" is only a metaphor for the totality of our humanity. The influence of Greek thinking on this expression tends to separate the terms mentioned into three distinct realms of human nature quite disconnected from each other, to be thought of as independent entities. If the Greeks had to picture this, they would draw the following diagram.

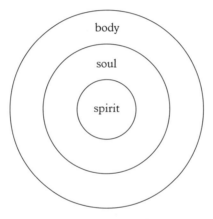

This drawing is quite contrary to Hebrew thinking, and some who want to separate themselves from this way of picturing human nature have tried to diagram the whole issue as follows:

Even this diagram is inadequate because it is impossible to lay out the different aspects of human nature like a cadaver on a table. One aspect of our human nature does not exist if any of the others don't. They are not entities separate from one another.

Instead, the Hebrews think of the "body" as a description of humanity in its totality, as viewed from a physical perspective. They similarly think of the "soul" as a description of humanity in its totality, but from the perspective of the way life was lived in all its humanness. Thus, the main focus is on the psychological aspects of living, how the self expressed itself in life intellectually, emotionally, and behaviorally. In a similar manner, Hebrews think of the "spirit" as a description of humanity in its totality, but this time from the perspective of spiritual realities, how the whole person interfaces with God, mainly through His Spirit. Thus, a more Hebrew way of picturing aspects of human nature would be like the following diagram.

| Body | Soul | Spirit |
|------|------|--------|
| The whole person from physical aspect | The whole person from human aspect | The whole person from spiritual aspect |

The fact remains, however, that Scripture often uses these three terms, either together or separately, and it behoves us to understand what is meant in their usage. This is dealt with more comprehensively in each of the following chapters. The central thrust of First Thessalonians 5:23 is to bring every aspect of our humanity, whichever way it is viewed, under the redeeming effects of the cross. We are to allow the cross to sanctify our bodies. We are to submit our soul to the redemptive and sanctifying effect of the same cross. And we are to do the same with our human spirit. What is more, we are to continue this practice constantly, until the coming of our Lord.

The encouraging thing is that the achievement of any desired level of holiness is not dependent on our ability or human effort to accomplish before we are accepted by God. The One who calls us is faithful, and "He will do it."

## MAKING USE OF WHAT GOD HAS REVEALED TO YOU IN ORDER TO BLESS HUMANITY

All of us wear spectacles of some sort as we look out onto the world and try to make sense of life around us. These philosophical glasses through which we interpret everything around us are usually called our "worldview." The apostle Paul warned us not to "conform…to the pattern of this world" (Rom. 12:2). He tells us that God can transform us by the renewing of our mind. Without God's help, most people find it almost impossible not to avoid adopting their own framework of meaning to live by.

Down through the Middle Ages, for example, the medieval church largely filtered out any human realities in the natural realms of relationships, psychology, and sociology, or the scientific realms of animals, plants, stars, or mathematics. The personal and impersonal realms of God and the spirit world of angels, demons, visions, dreams, witchcraft, sorcery, magic, and astrology had precedence for meaning over human sciences of any kind. Copernicus and Galileo were typical of scientists who never received a credible hearing for their discoveries.

In the pagan world of people in third world countries, the worldview was one of magic formulas. The realm of a personal God as Christians experienced him as Father, Jesus, and the Holy Spirit was replaced by impersonal "gods," karma, natural forces, gravity, the sun, and various forms of animal worship. Ceremonies, incantations, and shamanism were employed to control these gods for the benefit of worshipers.

With the rise of the enlightenment, an agnostic scientific rationalistic worldview gradually replaced that of the Middle Ages. The personal realms of psychology, sociology, and human relationships took precedence over the presence of a personal God and the spirit realm. The impersonal realm of scientific exploration assumed a focus largely ignored and feared in previous eras.

During the nineteenth century, a worldview of Deism arose among many evangelical Christians. A Deist is a person who believes in the existence of God somewhere in the distant universe but has dispatched Him to a far off place in such a way that He has no real personal interaction with us in the human experiences of our lives. The rationalistic, scientific mindset had heavily influenced this way of thinking about God. The Bible taught of God's existence, but His personal involvement in everyday life seemed distant or non-existent.

In the twentieth century, the barrenness of this type of Christianity could not be ignored. God in His providence created a longing for a much more authentic spirituality and the reality of the Holy Spirit and His availability to our humanity came to the fore. Many Christians these days are actually "recovering" Deists as they rediscover lost elements of the humanity that God has created them with. When buffeted by discouraging and destructive worldviews in the atmosphere of life that we all find saturate the world we live in, it is important to ground ourselves in the realities of life that God has shared with us in His Word.[4]

Let us now reflect in more detail on the way God strengthens and empowers us in the incredible humanity with which He has created us.

## ENDNOTES

1. H.E. Eusebius, (VII, xxv) and Tertullian (De carne Christi, xxiv).

2. Hans Kung, *Eternal Life?* (Garden City, N.Y.: Doubleday, 1984), 140.

3. Oscar Cullmann, *Immortality of the Soul or Resurrection of the Dead?* (London: Epworth Press, 1960), 14.

4. See the following helpful articles on the subject:

   ◆ Brian Knowles, "The Hebrew Mind versus the Western Mind";
   http://www.godward.org/Hebrew%20Roots/hebrew_mind_vs__the_western_mind.htm; accessed October 5, 2009.

   ◆ Nancy Scott, "Dueling with dualism";
   http://www.mckenziestudycenter.org/philosophy/articles/dualism.html; accessed October 5, 2009.

   ◆ George Eldon Ladd, "The Greek Versus the Hebrew View of Man";
   http://www.presenttruthmag.com/archive/XXIX/29-2.htm; accessed October 5, 2009.

   ◆ "Man as Body and Soul";
   http://www.presenttruthmag.com/archive/XXXVIII/38-3.htm; accessed October 5, 2009.

# CHAPTER TWO

# THE HUMAN BODY

# THE HUMAN BODY

*May your whole...body be kept blameless at the coming of our Lord Jesus Christ* (1 Thessalonians 5:23).

The Bible provides us with a clear description of how God's Word came to be written and its purpose for existence. "...Every part of Scripture is God-breathed and useful one way or another—showing us truth, exposing our rebellion, correcting our mistakes, training us to live God's way..." (2 Tim. 3:16 TM). I believe that except for a few isolated instances (for examples, the Ten Commandments,[1] the specific measurements for the original sanctuary,[2] and the letters to the seven churches in Asia Minor[3]), God did not dictate to its various writers the exact words He wanted us to read. At different times in history, God revealed Himself to individuals in order that His heart for humanity might be known. It was the person who was inspired by the Holy Spirit, rather than specific words. Each person wrote down the revelation he was given within the parameters of his own culture and the level of his education in a manner that was, nevertheless, guided by the Holy Spirit. This process is the same sort of intermingling that we witness in the mystery of Jesus Christ's humanity and divinity.

God's purpose in providing us with the Bible is clearly stated, "...training us to live God's way" (2 Tim. 3:16 TM). The Bible was written primarily as a guide book to salvation rather than an exact account of how everything in this world functions. We primarily needed to understand His standards of what is right, His acts that have made us right with Him again, and how we can live accordingly in a loving response to His goodness. The Bible is a book about personal relationships with a God who desires to enter into an intimate, personal covenant relationship with us. I don't think its purpose was to provide a scientific textbook on specific and extensive details of all matters of life on our planet.

## HUMAN NATURE IN THE EARLY CHAPTERS OF GENESIS

The first chapter of Genesis portrays God's heart for the human race. It only contained love and deep caring for His created beings. Everything He brought into existence prior to humankind's existence was done as a lavish gift that would provide for their every need, both practical, everyday requirements for basic living, and for their aesthetic enjoyment of beauty. The amazing spectrum of colors, tastes, smells, sounds, and texture was not an accident. The infinite diversity and thoughtfulness invested in every single thing, living or otherwise, were provided specifically to minister for our benefit. Modern nutritionists endorse that even the food given them to eat was extremely healthy. The statement that, "God saw all that He had made, and it was very good"[4] is the biggest understatement ever recorded.

The climax of creation was not humanity itself but human beings in relationship with God and each other. "God spoke, 'Let us make human beings in Our image, make them reflecting Our nature so they can be responsible for the fish in the sea, the birds in the air, the cattle, and, yes, Earth itself and every animal that moves on the face of Earth.' God created human beings; He created them godlike, reflecting God's nature. He created them male and female....'"[5]

## THE "IMAGE OF GOD"

What is meant by the term the *image of God* has long been debated. David Wilkinson has succinctly summarized five variant views below that scholars down through the ages have suggested this phrase, *the image of God*, means in his book, *The Message of Creation*.[6]

Audiani, in the fourth century, maintained that the "imago deo" embraced a physical image in some way. There are a few passages of Scripture that have been pressed to support this idea[7], but they are more likely descriptions of God in human terms to help people understand what God was trying to convey, expressions that have come to be known as *anthropomorphisms*. The Bible is very clear that God is Spirit and that we must worship Him as such, in our own human spirits[8] rather than in any concrete form. To worship God in any physical form is actually expressly forbidden in the second of the Ten Commandments.[9]

Augustine (A.D. 354-430) and Aquinas (A.D. 1225-74) suggested that the image of God encompassed the way humans, like God, could think. The phrase embraced a strong rationalistic emphasis and was very consistent with the rest of their theology which was firmly grounded on human reason.

A third school of thought focused on the freedom of humans to choose, to create things artistically, and to reproduce, as the essence of the image of God.

A fourth group pointed to the fact that God is holy and right in all His decisions, and has given humanity a similar sense of morality, even though in our present condition it is a long way from the nature and quality of God's morality.

The most convincing understanding of this term, however, comes out of a study of Genesis 1:26-27 in its context. There are two elements on which these verses focus. The first centers on the human role of "rulership" of the planet, which God had bestowed on the first man and woman as a divinely appointed responsibility. They were to be His representatives on earth and in so doing reflect His sovereignty over the whole universe.

This is echoed in the New Testament when on three occasions Jesus called satan, "the prince of this world." (See John 12:31; 14:30; 16:11.) In the second temptation in the wilderness, satan offered Jesus all the kingdoms of the world. "...I will give You all their authority and splendor, *for it has been given to me*, and I can give it to anyone I want to. So if You worship me, it will all be Yours" (Luke 4:6-7). Jesus did not contest

A LITTLE LOWER THAN THE ANGELS

satan's claim as legal, but made it clear that He had come to wrench those kingdoms out of his hand rather than receive them as a gift from satan (see Mark 3:22-27). Satan became the representative of planet Earth when Adam, the original God-appointed representative, surrendered it to God's adversary as described in Genesis 3:1-15. The Book of Job, accepted by most scholars as the oldest book in the Bible, even before Genesis, describes a time when satan had a limited, as that representative, access to Heaven after his fall. "…there was a day when the sons of God came to present themselves before the Lord, and Satan came also among them…" (Job 1:6-7 KJV).

It is no coincidence that Luke immediately followed his account of Jesus' baptism with a record of His genealogy, and intentionally ascribes this term, the "son of God," to Adam. The Father's voice had declared Jesus to be His own beloved Son. The genealogy deliberately applies the same term to Adam because he had no human being to call his father, but only God (see Luke 3:21-38). One of the characteristics of Luke's Gospel is that he consistently places emphasis on the humanity of Jesus. The point of the genealogy is that Jesus, as the new "Son of God" has come to take the place of Adam as the original "son of God." The apostle Paul calls Jesus the second Adam on several occasions (see Rom. 5:12-21; 1 Cor. 15:20-28).

The second aspect qualifying the "image of God" in the creation account is the relationship humans were to have, both with each other as male and female, and also to God Himself. God has never at any time existed in any sort of magnificent isolation. Even before any of the cosmos existed, He had always existed in relationship within Himself, a relationship that becomes clearer in the New Testament between God the Father, God the Son, and God the Holy Spirit (see John 14:16-17).

In some passages, God is portrayed as having characteristics usually described as feminine, traits such as care, nurture, and compassion (see Isa. 49:15; Matt. 23:37). In other passages He is portrayed as possessing distinctively male traits, such as warlikeness and protectiveness (see Jer 20:11). The primary significance of the maleness and femaleness of humanity, however, is that in their capacity to have a meaningful, intimate, and loving relationship with each other, they reflect the deepest essence of the image of God.

Considering all these possibilities about the meaning of the "image of God," it becomes evident that the first four do reflect elements of the essence of God in a limited way and, contradictory as it seems, that must include even our human bodies in some manner that we do not fully understand. Maybe the New Testament gets closest to it when it describes our body as a temple in which the Holy Spirit longs to dwell and fill with His living presence (see 1 Cor. 6:19-20).

What is very clear, however, is that Jesus is the only human who has reflected the image of God fully. "Anyone who has seen me," Jesus said to Philip, "has seen the Father." (See John 14:9; Hebrews 1:1-3.) Since the beginning of sin, we have actually become less human than God originally intended us to be. Sin has had a disastrous effect and has dehumanized us at the deepest level. Other than our first parents during their existence before sin entered the world, Jesus is the only person who was, and continues to be, fully human. He alone has an intimate relationship with God and has related in a similar loving way to other humans (see John 3:34, 10:30; Luke 3:21-22; Mark 6:34, 10:21). He, likewise, demonstrated His rulership over the elements of the earth (see Mark 4:35-41, 5:11-13, 6:30-51; Matthew 17:24-27). But it must also be acknowledged that He was also embodied, thought clearly, experienced emotions, exercised moral choices, and in so doing fleshed out all of the other aspects of the image of God previously mentioned.

## THE NATURE OF THE HUMAN BODY

The second chapter of Genesis gives further specific insights into various aspects of humanity. In an account of the creative process, the Bible says, "the Lord God formed the man from the dust of the ground and breathed into his nostrils the breath of life, and the man became a living being" (Gen. 2:7). With classical artistic flavor, God is portrayed as a potter molding Adam from elements of the earth. We are indeed formed from basic chemicals such as oxygen, carbon, hydrogen, nitrogen, and other minor elements, which return to the earth when we die (see Eccles. 12:7). Each of us has enough iron in our bodies to make several nails, enough calcium to paint a small chicken coup, and enough phosphorous to make a match. At this stage in Genesis, the human form, however, did not possess life in itself, so God breathed into the lifeless form the "breath of life" and man became a living being. The previously inert body now pulsed with the gift of life and began to function in all its humanity.

## THE IMPACT OF SIN

The third chapter of Genesis gives a vivid picture of the impact of sin on humanity. The first physical consequence that immediately became evident was that "...the eyes of both of them were opened, and they realized they were naked; so they sewed fig leaves together and made coverings for themselves" (Gen. 3:7). Prior to that time the record says, "The man and his wife were both naked, and they felt no shame" (Gen. 2:25). The sense of shame that emerged as the result of their choices became evident in two ways. They both tried to hide from each other and from God as He came looking for them in the cool of the evening. The selfless intimacy that existed in both of these two types of relationships was broken. The suggestion that their efforts to sew fig leaves together in order to cover themselves was evidence of sexual embarrassment and a primitive effort to cover their private parts is extremely problematic. More probable is the biblical emphasis on hiding from each other relationally, stemming from the wounds on their inner being that followed the impact of human sin.

The introduction of sin brought with it many other consequences that affected the human body. The earth brought forth thorns and thistles and had to be worked with "painful toil" to be productive. Women began an unfortunate experience of domination by men and pain in childbirth. These should not be interpreted in any way as a punishment by God for their part in the Fall, but rather a prophetic statement predicting the violation of women by men as yet another consequence that affected the human body down through the ages. Both the Old and New Testaments are a sad litany of male chauvinism with its consequent oppression and abuse of women.

The ultimate consequence of sin, however, is the universal destiny every person faces in death (see Gen. 2:15-17; Ps. 90:10). From the moment we are born, every human being commences to die. Some, like Abel, die prematurely from the evil actions of others, or by accident (see Gen. 4:8). Before this eventuality, however, it is the common lot of all humanity to experience the weaknesses and debilitations involved in growing old and the frailties of sickness and affliction (see Gen. 3:16-18; Eccles. 12:1-7). The body we have been given eventually returns to the ground from which its elements had originally been formed (see Gen. 2:7; Eccles. 12:7).

## CONTEMPORARY SCIENTIFIC INSIGHTS

Sir John Eccles (A.D. 1903-1997) was an Australian neurophysiologist who won the 1963 Nobel Prize in Physiology or Medicine for his work on synapses in the nerve endings of the human brain. He demonstrated that every thought and action sends a small electrical current down the axon from neurons in the brain to the synapse connecting it to the next neuron. That current can be measured at about 10 milli-volts, and is carried across the synapse by neurotransmitters. Eccles studied the synapses under a microscope and noticed small nodules imbedded in the ganglia of each synapse. Because they looked like buttons, he named them by the French word *buton*. He also noted that the more a person thought, spoke, or did anything, the larger the butons became in size and the more they grew in number. And they could never be removed. Eccles realized that he was looking at the basis of human habit, and that thoughts and actions are physiologically embedded in our brains in such a way that habits become deeply ingrained and irreversible.

That sounds very discouraging, if it were not for the fact that the human brain has far more neurons than it ever uses. If addicted individuals choose to form a new habit, new neurons are developed in the same synapse and new butons are awakened. The brain has a remarkable mechanism by which the old butons can be repressed if choices are made to start a new habit. A chemical called gaba is pumped into the synaptic connection with the old butons, which represses their influence, and another chemical

35

called acetylcholine is pumped into the synaptic connection with the new butons that enables them to function successfully. The old butons, however, still remain dormant and are stimulated immediately if they are re-activated. This explains why an alcoholic can be a non-drinking alcoholic, but the moment he or she takes one drink the alcoholic pattern immediately reasserts its dominance.[10]

## DEMONIC INFLUENCES ON THE HUMAN BODY

Scripture indicates that if the way God created us to live is abused or a person's spiritual sensitivity is violated, then the door for demonic influences is opened on that person. If the influence is not initially resisted and dealt with properly through the counsel Paul gave in Ephesians 6:10-18, then demonic activity deepens to a level of oppression. It appears that this was the experience of King Saul when he would call for David to play music for him (see James 4:7; 1 Sam. 18:10-11). The final and ultimate activity of satan is one of possession, when he takes up residence within a human being. The demoniac of Gadara is a classic example of the impact of demon possession on a person's body. Mark records how, "This man lived in the tombs, and no one could bind him any more, not even with a chain. For he had often been chained hand and foot, but he tore the chains apart and broke the irons on his feet. No one was strong enough to subdue him. Night and day among the tombs and in the hills he would cry out and cut himself with stones" (Mark 5:3-5).

It appears, however, that demons cannot take possession of a human body unless the individual gives them some access to do so and fosters that access. Paul describes the parts of our body as instruments for righteousness or unrighteousness. "...Do not offer the parts of your body to sin, as instruments of wickedness," he says, "but rather offer yourselves to God, as those who have been brought from death to life; and offer the parts of your body to him as instruments of righteousness..." (Rom. 6:13). We have the choice to use our body whichever way we decide.

## ENDNOTES

1.  See Exodus 20.

2.  See Exodus 25–30.

3.  See Revelation 2–3.

4.  See Genesis 1:31.

5.  See Genesis 1:26-27 TM.

6.  David Wilkinson, *The Message of Creation* (Leicester, UK: InterVarsity Press, 2000), 34-38.

7.  See Exodus 33:21; Daniel 7:9-10.

8.  See John 4:24.

9.  See Exodus 20:4-6.

10. *Nobel Lectures, Physiology or Medicine: 1963-1970*, (Amsterdam, NL: Elsevier Publishing Company, 1972).

# CHAPTER THREE

# JESUS' HUMAN BODY

# JESUS' HUMAN BODY

The birth of Jesus presents us with aspects of His nature that, although stated matter-of-factly and unambiguously, are still difficult for us to comprehend in all their fullness. In the ultimate sense, our faith in these realities is based on historical facts revealed in Scripture rather than any total comprehensive human understanding.

The angel Gabriel came to Mary and shared with her the circumstances of Jesus' impending birth. "'Good morning! You're beautiful with God's beauty, beautiful inside and out! God be with you.' She was thoroughly shaken, wondering what was behind a greeting like that. But the angel assured her, 'Mary, you have nothing to fear. God has a surprise for you; you will become pregnant and give birth to a Son and call His name Jesus. He will be great, and will be called "Son of the Highest." The Lord God will give Him the throne of His father David; He will rule Jacob's house forever—no end, ever, to His Kingdom.' Mary said to the angel, 'But how? I've never slept with a man.' The angel answered, 'The Holy Spirit will come upon you; the power of the Highest will hover over you. Therefore, the child you bring to birth will be called Holy, Son of God. And did you know that your cousin Elizabeth conceived a son, old as she is? Everyone called her barren, and here she is six months pregnant! Nothing, you see, is impossible with God.' And Mary said, 'Yes, I see it all now; I'm the Lord's maid, ready to serve. Let it be with me just as you say.' Then the angel left her." (See Luke 1:28-38.)

The Scripture is categorical that Jesus' conception was not the result of any human cohabitation. The embryonic seed was placed in Mary's womb by the Holy Spirit rather than Joseph. This is confirmed by Joseph's initial decision to break his betrothal to her upon hearing the news of her pregnancy. It was only on the intervention of Gabriel himself that Joseph, obviously a godly man, accepted the reality of what had happened and supported Mary in her journey throughout life, one that constantly bore the stigma of Jesus'"illegitimacy" (see Matt. 1:18-25; John 9:29).

It is clear from these verses, however, that although Jesus received His humanity from Mary, His divinity was transmitted through the Holy Spirit. These two aspects of His nature coexisted in a unique blending and will continue to do so for the rest of eternity (see Phil. 3:20-21; Heb. 7:24 KJV). It is also clear from the limited revelation of Jesus' childhood that He developed as a human being the way all human beings do. It is recorded that "…the child grew and became strong; He was filled with wisdom, and the grace of God was upon Him" and "…Jesus grew in wisdom and stature, and in favor with God and men" (Luke 2:40,52). These verses imply a harmonious and comprehensive development in Jesus' formative years in all areas of His humanity: physically, socially, intellectually, and spiritually.

It is interesting to reflect on how and when Jesus became aware of His divinity. This can only be a matter of conjecture, but the Scripture is clear that by the age of twelve, He had developed a clear understanding of who His real Father was and what sacrificial destiny lay ahead of Him (see Luke 2:41-49). We can only surmise that maybe His mother had told Him of the circumstances concerning his birth. Certainly, like any Jewish boy growing up in a Hebrew village, He would have spent much time studying the Scriptures in the local synagogue. That being the case, the Holy Spirit would have illumined His mind and spirit concerning the Messianic prophecies. His first visit to Jerusalem, predictably at twelve years of age for His bar-mitzvah, would have confronted Him with the sacrifices offered up in the temple courts and underscored His ultimate future for the whole human race.

It is not until His baptism at the river Jordan, however, that there is the first written record of God the Father speaking to Him audibly and confirming His identity with the words, "…You are my Son, whom I love; with You I am well pleased" (Luke 3:22). It is as if the Father was saying to the human Jesus, "What you have taken by faith for the first thirty years of Your life is a fact. You are My Son…and I love you."

There is, however, one fundamental difference between the humanity of Jesus and our existence as humans today. The angel said to Mary, "The Holy Spirit will come upon you, and the power of the Most High will cover you. For this reason the baby will be holy and will be called the Son of God" (Luke 1:35 NCV). The King James Version calls the baby "that holy thing which shall be born of thee." This is a focus on the holiness, and by implication, the sinlessness of Jesus. Jesus, unlike us, was born without sin residing "in" the propensities of His human nature. He, moreover, continued to live as such throughout His life. In contrast, David identified with the whole human race when he said of himself, "Surely I was sinful at birth, sinful from the time my mother conceived me" (Ps. 51:5). By that he did not mean he was born illegitimately. He was saying that from the moment of his conception he, and every human being, had inclinations and propensities to sin in his behavior because an inherited power of sinfulness resided intrinsically in human nature and had been passed down to him along with every man and woman.

## THE NATURE OF SIN AND ITS IMPACT
## ON THE HUMAN BODY

We have reflected somewhat briefly on the impact of sin on our humanity. But it is necessary to emphasize the truly radical effect sin has on every aspect of our being. It began in the area of Adam and Eve's relationship with God before they ever committed a sinful act. The serpent challenged God's word concerning the consequences of eating from the tree of the knowledge of good and evil (see Gen. 3:1-4). The couple were thrown into a position of having to choose whom they would trust. Would they trust God's word for them or the word of the deceiver? Thought of in this sense, sin is primarily a distrust of God and His Word, the Bible. It is a decision to live independent from God and His counsel, and in essence rebel against His lordship and sovereignty (see Rom. 14:23).

Only then, did sin manifest itself in behavior. They partook of the fruit and ate it. There is no way that we can describe this second aspect of sin other than disobedience. It was a transgression of His stated requirement of them, of His divine law (see 1 John 3:4).

But we must not stop here at mere behavior. Sin has a far more radical consequence than our actions. At that fateful moment, something changed deeply within human nature. Our minds became confused and we could no longer think clearly. Our emotions became alienated from God and each other. Our will chose things outside the will of God and became impotent to fully obey His requirements or His heart. Sin became like a cancer eating away at every noble aspect of our inner being in such a way that we were permanently sick, dying, and could never heal ourselves (see Jer. 17:9).

Jesus made that categorically clear when He said, "What comes out of a man is what makes him 'unclean.' For from within, out of men's hearts, come evil thoughts, sexual immorality, theft, murder, adultery, greed, malice, deceit, lewdness, envy, slander, arrogance and folly. All these evils come from inside and make a man 'unclean'" (Mark 7:20-23).

James underlines the same truth when he says that when tempted, no one should say, "Don't let anyone under pressure to give in to evil say, 'God is trying to trip me up.' God is impervious to evil, and puts evil in no one's way. The temptation to give in to evil comes from us and only us. We have no one to blame but the leering, seducing flare-up of our own lust. Lust gets pregnant, and has a baby: sin! Sin grows up to adulthood, and becomes a real killer" (James 1:13-15 TM).

And should we still be in doubt of how God regards our basic human nature, there is no way we can escape the confronting collection of quotes from the Old Testament. These quotes, pulled together by Paul in the following verses, describe this radically deep third aspect of sin residual in our human nature until the final day of history, when God deals with it conclusively at the culmination of Christ's work on the cross—when He comes a second time (see Rom. 8:22-23; 1 Cor. 15:51-54).

> *So where does that put us? Do we Jews get a better break than the others? Not really. Basically, all of us, whether insiders or outsiders, start out in identical conditions, which is to say that we all start out as sinners. Scripture leaves no doubt about it: There's nobody living right, not even one, nobody who knows the score, nobody alert for God. They've all taken the wrong turn; they've all wandered down blind alleys. No one's living right; I can't find a single one. Their throats are gaping graves, their tongues slick as mud slides. Every word they speak is tinged with poison. They open their mouths and pollute the air. They race for the honor of sinner-of-the-year, litter the land with heartbreak and ruin, Don't know the first thing about living with others. They never give God the time of day. This makes it clear, doesn't it, that whatever is written in these Scriptures is not what God says about others but to us to whom these Scriptures were addressed in the first place! And it's clear enough, isn't it, that we're sinners, every one of us, in the same sinking boat with everybody else? Our involvement with God's revelation doesn't put us right with God. What it does is force us to face our complicity in everyone else's sin* (Romans 3:9-20 TM).

Some have wondered whether the fact that Jesus had a sinless inner human nature may have disqualified Him from being our Savior. Would that mean that He had an advantage over us and never faced all the types of temptations that we in our sinful humanity have to face? This is not a simple question because there are two issues at stake in the temptations that Jesus experienced.

In one sense there were some temptations that Jesus could not have experienced in a literal manner. As a young, free, Jewish male, He could never have experienced many of the specific temptations unique to women, husbands, the aged, slaves, or Gentiles.

Having recognized this, however, He certainly would have experienced all the temptations these people have gone through in their lives, yet in different circumstances. Jesus could never have been betrayed as a husband, for example, but He certainly experienced betrayal in a different context and would have understood the deep pain involved in every form of betrayal. Despite such betrayal, He never responded sinfully. The writer of the Book of Hebrews expresses this thought when he says, "…We don't have a priest who is out of touch with our reality. He's been through weakness and testing, experienced it all—all but the sin…" (Heb. 4:15 TM).

In a totally different sense, however, the temptations Jesus experienced were very different and quite unique to all human beings except Adam and Eve. Satan recognized that Jesus had actually come to earth fully human in order to fill a specific role as a new representative of the human race to replace Adam (see Matt 4:8-11; John 12:31; 14:30; 16:11). Adam and Eve fell into sin while they were still sinless. Sin actually dehumanized them, and as a consequence, every human being that issued from them. We are all now less than truly human and Jesus, in His sinlessness, is the only model we have of true humanity as God created it and desires us to be. Paul calls Jesus the second Adam (see Rom. 5:12-19; 1 Cor. 15:20-28).

The type of temptations satan directed at Jesus were the very ones our original parents faced. We have already noticed that they, while sinless, were tempted to distrust God and disobey Him. The medium used to clarify their trust or distrust centered on diet—whether they should eat or not eat the fruit from the tree of the knowledge of good and evil (see Gen. 2:15-17). They chose to distrust Him, and the consequences are well-known.

In all of Jesus' temptations, the central issues He faced were exactly the same as those directed to Adam. The description of His first major temptation (see Luke 4:1-13) describes how He was challenged to turn stones into bread after not eating for forty days. In a similar manner, satan sought to entice Him to use His divine power to save Himself from hunger, struggle, and presumption. Had He done so, Jesus would have forsaken His sinless humanity by taking up His divinity and therefore disqualifying Himself from being our corporate representative human being before the Father. None of us in our humanity are capable of doing the things satan asked of Jesus during those forty days in the wilderness.

Even on the cross of Calvary, satan pushed Jesus in a game of brinkmanship to its limit. In the mocking sneers of the chief priests, the teachers of the law, the Jewish elders, the soldiers, and the dying thieves beside Him, satan pressed Jesus to forget His plan of salvation and return to Heaven. This would have been an almost overpowering temptation for Jesus. In the garden of Gethsemane, He had asked God to save Him from death on the cross (see Matt. 26:39).

No humans seemed to be responding to what Jesus was doing for their salvation, and the enemy was tempting Him to feel that it was all pointless. "'He saved others,' they [religious leaders] said, 'but He can't save Himself! He's the King of Israel! Let Him come down now from the cross, and we will believe in Him. He trusts in God. Let God rescue Him now if He wants Him, for He said, "I am the Son of God."' In the same way the robbers who were crucified with Him also heaped insults on Him" (Matt. 27:41-44).

Jesus was fully capable of coming down from the cross and going back to Heaven (see Matt 26:52-53). Had He done so, the whole human race would have been lost for eternity. It defies comprehension that He was willing to endure separation from His Father, from whom He had earlier felt forsaken (see Matt. 27:46), in order to give us eternal life. This is the definitive measuring stick of God's love for us in its nature and magnitude.

It is summed up adequately by the writer to the Hebrews when he said, "...We don't have a priest who is out of touch with our reality. He's been through weakness and testing, experienced it all—all but the sin..." (Heb. 4:15 TM). Thoughtful reflection on this verse of Scripture reveals that Jesus was tempted in every way true humanity was tested by satan in the beginning, yet unlike Adam, Jesus maintained His sinlessness.

There is one sense, however, in which the physical body of Jesus had been outwardly impacted by sin. He was born into a world that had been ravaged physically by the consequences of sin. The stories from Genesis portray human beings who lived for much longer periods of time than we do today and were more robust in their stature. Jesus inherited a human body from Mary that bore all the consequences of sin from the time of creation (see Phil. 2:6-8). That would have made His temptations infinitely more acute, considering the pristine physical condition of Adam at the time of his similar temptations.

A consideration of how Jesus took a human body at His birth, suffered in a human body at His death, and assumed a human body forever at His resurrection, is a profound statement of the value God places on the human body. It underscores the counsel He has included in Scripture for the care of the human body and the value He placed on it in the Kingdom of God.

# CHAPTER FOUR

# THE HUMAN BODY
# AND THE COMING
# OF GOD'S KINGDOM

# THE HUMAN BODY
# AND THE COMING
# OF GOD'S KINGDOM

The central message of Jesus was that He came to usher in the Kingdom of God, the rulership of God in this world instead of the rulership of satan. Prior to this time, Paul describes all who had not entered into a covenant with God as those who follow "...the ways of this world and of the ruler of the kingdom of the air, the spirit who is now at work in those who are disobedient. All of us also lived among them at one time, gratifying the cravings of our sinful nature and following its desires and thoughts" (Eph. 2:2-3).

To emphasize the significance of His ministry, Jesus forcefully proclaimed, "The time has come...The kingdom of God is near. Repent and believe the good news! ...Come, follow me..." (Mark 1:15,17). To reinforce His words, Jesus gave evidence of the presence of the Kingdom of God by healing diseases, casting out demons and raising people from the dead. These miracles were not themselves the essence of the Kingdom of God, but rather signs that the Kingdom of God had indeed come in the person of Jesus. Jesus was revealing to all that desired to see, that He had the intention and ability to restore His creation to its original condition. The fullest manifestation of that will transpire at the end of time when "...in keeping with His promise we are looking forward to a new heaven and a new earth, the home of righteousness" (2 Peter 3:13). It is a sad comment on human history that the Christian Church, made up as it is of imperfect human beings, has taken such a long time to manifest the reality of the presence of the Kingdom of God in all areas of race, gender, and social discrimination. Jesus not only launched His Kingdom, He modeled it in these issues as a legacy for all of us to fulfill (see Gal. 3:26-29).

## JESUS' PHYSICAL HUMAN BODY—A SYMBOL OF CHRISTIAN LIFE

One last thing needs to be said in our reflections on the human body. The Greek philosophers almost had it right in one sense when they said matter was only a shadow of the spirit realm. God actually does use things in the material world to illustrate spiritual principles. The big difference is that He doesn't negate the reality and basic goodness of the material world in order to do so. All nature that came lovingly from His hand is used in some way as a tableau of God's heart and purposes for us.

Jesus was a master at doing this in His parables. In His parables, He was in all probability pointing to live actualities either in front of Him, or with which everybody was familiar. Shepherds were everywhere in Palestine; in telling the parable of the Good Shepherd, He was in effect saying, "Look at that shepherd over there. He is real enough. But I want you to also think about how I am your Shepherd and care for you in exactly the same way that shepherd cares for his sheep" (see John 10:1-18). He did the same thing with everything that existed: gates, doors, vines, gardeners, soils, seeds, bread, water, wine, light, mother hens, fig trees, temples, fish, and on and on.

By far, the most significant metaphors He used were drawn from the human body. The manner in which different church members were to relate to each other and function in their spiritual gifts without manifestations of superiority or inferiority is likened to the marvelous unity and interaction of different members of the human body (see 1 Cor. 12:12-31).

In a more personal sense, Jesus used the metaphors of birth and marital intimacy to bring awareness of lessons He wanted us to grasp about His relationship with us. It's as if He were seeking to say things such as, "When you hold your newly born child in your arms for the first time and experience the magnitude of parental love welling up in your heart, can't you see that I have given you this experience on a human level in order to open your heart to realize how much I, as your heavenly parent, love you infinitely more (see Luke 15:11-32; 18:15-17). And don't you see that when as a couple you lie together in the intimacy of your marriage relationship, I am trying to open to you in the intensity of your own human experience how much I want to have union with you. I want to enter into you, leave my seed in you, and reproduce myself in you." To emphasize this, Jesus told many parables about weddings. He is the Bridegroom and we are His Bride. Biblical scholars have built a whole cohesive theology of the Bible on this theme. The covenant we enter into with our partner in marriage is modeled on the covenant He enters into with us for our salvation (see John 2:1-11; Matt. 22:1-14; Rev. 19:6-9).

The clearest teaching on this subject comes in the Book of Ephesians.

> *Submit to one another out of reverence for Christ. Wives, submit to your husbands as to the Lord. For the husband is the head of the wife as Christ is the head of the church, His body, of which He is the Savior. Now as the church submits to Christ, so also wives should submit to their husbands in everything. Husbands, love your wives, just as Christ loved the church and gave Himself up for her to make her holy, cleansing her by the washing with water through the word, and to present her to Himself as a radiant church, without stain or wrinkle or any other blemish, but holy and blameless. In this same way, husbands ought to love their wives as their own bodies. He who loves his wife loves himself. After all, no one ever hated his own body, but he feeds and cares for it, just as Christ does the church—for we are members of His body. "For this reason a man will leave his father and mother and be united to his wife, and the two will become one flesh." This is a profound mystery—but I am talking about Christ and the church"* (Ephesians 5:21-32).

In the second half of the Book of Ephesians, Paul is applying the practical outworking of what it means to be "in Christ" to various situations of everyday life. The Ephesians 5:21-32 passage empha-sizes that to be "in Christ" requires a mutual submission of husband and wife to each another in their marriage, and this is spelled out in detail in the cultural traditions of Paul's day. It must be emphasized that the word *submission* does not imply a compulsory servile capit-ulation. The manner in which wives are called upon to voluntarily submit themselves in love and respect to their husbands was to be modeled on the way all Christians submit to Jesus. To do so ex-pressed an inner attitude that echoes the Christians' response to all that Jesus has done for them in provision and protection.

The model given to husbands to voluntarily submit themselves in love and respect to their wives, is the way Christ loves the Church. He selflessly gave everything to save His bride. The one concern of every husband should be to do everything possible to encourage his wife in her journey toward Heaven, to help her become blameless and spotless in the eyes of Jesus, and to do nothing that would be a stumbling block to her salvation. It uses the classic spiritual model of Jesus as the spiritual Bridegroom and the church as His spiritual Bride. Paul says that this metaphor is the mystery, or revealed mean-ing, of human marriage.

It seems clear that the human body and the human soul and the human spirit can be distinguished from one another, and are differ-ent ways of reflecting on the totality of our humanity. We must real-ize, however, that they should never be separated into any Greek type of unrelated compartments. Each aspect of our human nature is intimately involved in a concrete unity. What affects the one is in-extricably intertwined with the others and invariably affects them in their everyday function. And because of this, it is also not hard to realize, then, why the human body and the way we use it becomes satan's prime target of dehumanization. Our collective record as human beings in self-indulgence, gluttony, sexual depravity, abuse, and destruction of other human bodies defies imagination. The Bible describes violation of our trust in these areas as characteristic of life at the end of this present age. (See Revelation 11:16-18, 22:12-15; 2 Timothy 3:1-7; Romans 1:18-32.)

## BIBLICAL GUIDELINES FOR THE CARE OF YOUR BODY

Despite all the degenerating and destructive influences of sin on our human frame, the Bible calls for respect of the body. There is ample counsel given in the Word of God to matters of health, general hygiene, diet, and sexuality. Following the Exodus from Egypt, God saw that it was necessary to instruct and train the Israelite nation in these matters before they entered Canaan to prevent any of the diseases that were so prevalent during their experience of slavery (see Exod. 15:26).

There is much wisdom in this ancient writing that is still very applicable to developing countries in our modern world today. Every individual who came in contact with contagious diseases was isolated from the camp and not allowed to return without effective cleansing of his or her body and clothing (see Lev. 15:4-12). Leprosy was a common disease encountered in the Middle East at that time and received special attention (see Lev. 13:46-52). Any house that was considered unsafe for occupation was to be totally destroyed (see Lev. 14:45-47). Sanitation was ensured by strict orders to remove all refuse from the camp (see Deut. 23:12-14). It was especially necessary in a hot desert environment that issues of blood needed to be addressed for the sake of hygiene (see Lev. 15). In matters of diet, many guidelines were given to ensure the best nutrition available at the time (see Gen. 1:29, 3:18; Lev. 11:1-47; 1 Cor. 10:31). The distinction between clean and unclean foods was not initially or primarily given to the Jewish nation for ceremonial purposes alone. These particular guidelines preceded the formation of the nation of Israel (see Gen. 7:1-5) and had as their main purpose principles of health. All prohibited animals, fish, and birds fell into the category of scavengers. These laws were a rule of thumb providing guidelines as to what was healthy and what wasn't for people who were not as aware of nutrition as we are today.

Many warnings were given throughout Scripture regarding problems related to alcohol (see Gen. 9:18-27; Prov. 23:29-35; 1 Cor. 5:11; Rev. 22), and these principles can be extended to all forms of harmful drugs and mind-destroying narcotics.

Prohibition concerning certain sexual relationships and practices did not arise out of overly prim and prudish attitudes characteristic of the Victorian period during the late 1800s. The Principles shared within the Bible were given by a loving God who understands the consequences of genetic inbreeding and the protection of the family from moral disintegration (see Lev. 18). Sexuality was not considered dirty or sinful by the Hebrews. The Book Song of Solomon is a sacred song generally believed to be sung in the background of wedding festivities, celebrating the beauty of love and the joys of intimacy between a husband and wife in marriage.

## BODY HEALTH IN THE NEW TESTAMENT

By the time of Jesus, the Jewish nation had lost sight of the intrinsic purpose of the Levitical laws regarding these types of health issues and had turned them into a mechanism of earning merit with God. At the same time, their sense of racial superiority and their fetish for approaching these laws legalistically made them objectionable to surrounding nations (see Rom. 2:24) and unfortunately served only to separate them from their cultural neighbors rather than being a blessing for all humanity.

This trend began when the Jewish exiles returned from their captivity in Babylon under the leadership of Ezra and Nehemiah around 450 B.C. (see Ezra 1:1-4; Neh. 2:1-11). The nation came to realize that it was their failure to keep a covenantal relationship with God that had led them into captivity in the first place. Instead of seeing that as a statement concerning a failure of their heart relationship with God, they interpreted it as a failure to keep Levitical laws properly and began a long process of adding a multitude of other restrictions, rules, and "laws" to be interpreted and kept. The Pharisees in Jesus' day had developed this into a fine art. Their commentaries on the Scripture on these matters (the Talmud) stand as a witness to the blind alley of legalism in these areas. The practices and attitudes that isolated them from other nations assumed a quality of disdain and arrogance that ultimately made relationships with any non-Jew almost impossible (see Mark 7:1-8, 24-30; Acts 10:1-11; Acts 11:1-18; Gal. 2:11-21).

The Jewish response to Peter's extended visit to the home of Cornelius (a non-Jewish Gentile) was characteristic of most Jewish people. They would not relate to Gentiles because they believed it would make them ceremoniously "unclean" and disqualify them to participate in many Jewish rites and activities. It was understandable that many Gentiles felt rejected and classified as second rate people by this behavior, which was essentially arrogant elitism and prejudice. Over a period of time, these attitudes created deep-seated resentments between the races. (See John 4:9 and Romans 14:1-4.)

Jesus addressed these attitudes head on, and in so doing, confronted the heart of their ethnic conceit and false understanding of how to get right with God. His pointed emphasis created such deeply ingrained hostility from the religious leadership that it ultimately culminated in His death. In His homecoming address to the synagogue at Nazareth, for example, He provocatively pointed out that "…there were many widows in Israel in Elijah's time, when the sky was shut for three and a half years and there was a severe famine throughout the land. Yet Elijah was not sent to any of them, but to a widow in Zarephath in the region of Sidon, a port on the Mediterranean Sea in modern Lebanon. "And there were many in Israel with leprosy in the time of Elisha the prophet, yet not one of them was cleansed—only Naaman the Syrian" (Luke 4:25-27). The prejudiced worshipers reacted with such fury that they tried to kill Him by seeking to push Him over a cliff.

On another occasion,

> *…Jesus called the crowd to Him and said, "Listen to me, everyone, and understand this. Nothing outside a man can make him 'unclean' by going into him. Rather, it is what comes out of a man that makes him 'unclean.'" After He had left the crowd and entered the house, His disciples asked Him about this parable. "Are you so dull?" He asked. "Don't you see that nothing that enters a man from the outside can make him 'unclean'? For it doesn't go into his heart but into his stomach, and then out of his body." (In saying this, Jesus declared all foods "clean.") He went on: "What comes out of a man is what makes him 'unclean.' For from within, out of men's hearts,*

*come evil thoughts, sexual immorality, theft, murder, adultery, greed, malice, deceit, lewdness, envy, slander, arrogance and folly. All these evils come from inside and make a man 'unclean'"* (Mark 7:14-23).

It is self-evident, however, that if the foods previously classified in the Old Testament as unclean were labelled as such for health reasons, then their nutritional value did not change with Christ's pronouncement. The Old Testament guidelines for what is and what is not healthy to eat still remain valid. Jesus was addressing the false theology and hypocrisy of Judaism that sought to turn such guidelines into a way of justifying themselves before God as a gateway to Heaven and in so doing excluding other nations from the same destiny.

The New Testament does not ignore guidelines for health in any way (see 3 John 2). It, in fact, raises the bar by giving such guidelines a spiritual component. Christians were to regard their bodies as a temple of the Holy Spirit and put into them only those things that did not impinge on or detract from their spiritual discernment. They were to choose those foods that were the healthiest available and so bring glory to God. Nor were those things to purposely erect a barrier between other human beings as had been previously the case. In addressing the matter of whether to eat food that had been previously sacrificed to pagan idols, Paul said, "'Everything is permissible'—but not everything is beneficial. 'Everything is permissible'—but not everything is constructive...So whether you eat or drink or whatever you do, do it all for the glory of God" (1 Cor. 10:23,31).

The same advice was given to the Gentile and Jewish Christians in Rome who had difficulty living and worshiping with each other as a result of the lingering dynamics of their deeply established previous heritage. Jews and Gentiles were to think their convictions through as best they could, be true to what they were convinced of in all faith, and cease condemning the group who adopted any opposite or differing alternative. At the same time, Paul clearly identified himself with the "strong" Gentile Christians who were not bound, as were the weak Hebrew Christians, by their past heritage. Whatever their decision, they were all urged to recognize that "...the kingdom of God is not a matter of eating and drinking, but of righteousness, peace and joy in the Holy Spirit, because anyone who serves Christ in this way is pleasing to God and approved by men" (Rom. 14:17-18).

The definitive statement from the newly born Christian church on all these issues was drawn up at their first church council held in Jerusalem and recorded in Acts 15. This meeting of church leaders had been called specifically to clarify whether or not Gentiles should embrace the requirements of Hebrew law before they became bona fide Christians. After hearing from several apostles how God had already short-circuited such requirements by pouring out the Holy Spirit on Gentiles who believed in Jesus, the church representatives summarized their conclusions. Instructions were sent to all the churches that, "It seemed good to the Holy Spirit and to us not to burden you with anything beyond the following requirements: You are to abstain from food sacrificed to idols, from blood, from the meat of strangled animals and from sexual immorality. You will do well to avoid these things" (Acts 15:28-29). It has even been suggested that some of these caveats limited an absolute total freedom in Christ and may have been included for the purpose of considering Jewish sensitivities in the overall fellowship of all Christians.

The spiritual connection given in the New Testament to the way Christians treat their bodies and what they ingest into them, serves to clarify a number of other practices that are spoken of in Scripture. Fasting, for example, has always been an exercise in Christian tradition to heighten spiritual awareness and sensitivity. When Jesus began His ministry following His baptism, the record says that the Holy Spirit drew Him out into the desert to fast for a period of forty days in order to prepare for the times that lay ahead. The desert provided an environment that avoided the stimuli of cities and crowds of people. It has also been shown that the abstinence of food allows clarity of mental and spiritual perception. The Holy Spirit is able to connect with the fine nerve fibres of our brain and download from God any communication with us into a body and system that is more receptive under these conditions.

It is obvious that any drug, narcotic or drink that chemically affects the brain is going to hamper the Holy Spirit's ability to communicate with us, and why the Bible regards violation of awareness in these areas as an act of spiritual sabotage. The opposite is also true. The faithfulness of Daniel and his three friends in matters of diet and beverages while they were captives in Nebuchadnezzar's palace and being trained for service in his court, appears to be the main reason why God was able to invest them with the spiritual integrity and prophetic giftings they manifested in subsequent times (see Dan. 1).

# Chapter Five

# GOD'S REVEALED
# WISDOM

# GOD'S REVEALED WISDOM

As Christians we must never forget the value God places on our body. Let me ask you personally, "How does He do this for you individually?"

First, He has created your body exactly as it is, with all the wonder and attractiveness it has and also any features that may have become marred for any reason. "Then God said, 'Let us make man in Our image, in Our likeness, and let them rule over the fish of the sea and the birds of the air, over the livestock, over all the earth, and over all the creatures that move along the ground.' So God created man in His own image, in the image of God He created him; male and female He created them" (Gen. 1:26-27).

There are some texts in the Bible that do seem to indicate that we reflect some aspect of a physical image of God. Speaking to Moses, God said, "When my glory passes by, I will put you in a cleft in the rock and cover you with My hand until I have passed by. Then I will remove My hand and you will see My back; but My face must not be seen" (Exod. 33:22-23).

In describing a vision of God sitting in judgment, the prophet Daniel portrays Him as follows: "As I looked, 'thrones were set in place, and the Ancient of Days took His seat. His clothing was as white as snow; the hair of His head was white like wool...'" (Dan. 7:9).

We must never forget, however, that God is not in any way like us. The apostle John says, "God is spirit, and His worshipers must worship in spirit and in truth" (John 4:24).

The Bible constantly reminds us that we are never to represent God in any material mode as an aid to worship and unconsciously bring Him down to our absolute level. "You shall not make for yourself an idol in the form of anything in heaven above or on the earth beneath or in the waters below. You shall not bow down to them or worship them…" (Exod. 20:4-5).

Ascribing God in physical terms, as in these passages, are only literary symbols to help us understand His care for us in human terms. These expressions are given the technical term *anthropomorphisms*.

From the very beginning of recorded history, God has always delighted in us as human beings. We were the climax of His creative work. Everything in the first chapter of Genesis that God created was a preamble to our existence and specifically designed by God to minister to our physical, psychological, and spiritual needs. It was as if He was rolling out the red carpet preparing for our arrival. And nothing in this preliminary provision was shabby or second rate in any way. He could have created every color a dull gray. Every taste could have been unpleasantly bitter. Every smell could have been a stench. Every texture could have been like a stinging nettle and every sound a cacophony. And yet it was exactly the opposite. His whole creative work was lavish and prodigal in its color, taste, sound, feel, and fragrance. The psalmist tells us that God put more individual thought into the creation of each one of us than there are grains of sand in the sea.

*How precious to me are your thoughts, O God! How vast is the sum of them! Were I to count them, they would outnumber the grains of sand…* (Psalm 139:17-18).

*For You created my inmost being; You knit me together in my mother's womb. I praise You because I am fearfully and wonderfully made; Your works are wonderful, I know that full well. My frame was not hidden from You when I was made in the secret place. When I was woven together in the depths of the earth, Your eyes saw my unformed body. All the days ordained for me were written in Your book before one of them came to be* (Psalm 139:13-16).

Nor did He hide Himself from us, even in our rebellion against Him. He came searching for us in the cool of the day instead of the heat of the day full of anger (see Gen. 3:8-9). The Bible is not the story of humankind searching after God—it is the very reverse; God searching after humankind.

*When I consider Your heavens, the work of Your fingers, the moon and the stars, which You have set in place, what is man that You are mindful of him, the son of man that You care for him? You made him a little lower than the heavenly beings and crowned him with glory and honor. You made him ruler over the works of Your hands; You put everything under his feet: all flocks and herds, and the beasts of the field, the birds of the air, and the fish of the sea, all that swim the paths of the seas* (Psalm 8:3-8).

Despite this reality about His essentially spiritual nature, God has still chosen to create us physically and corporeally. Unlike the Greek philosophers, He does not despise matter. When Jesus was on earth, He constantly used the physical realities of our lives to illustrate spiritual principles. The intimacy we have with each other in marriage, for example, opens our eyes to the unity He desires to have with us in our spirit. He calls himself our Bridegroom and us His Bride. As we hold our children in our arms, our roles as mothers and fathers open our eyes to His fatherhood of us as His children. The shepherds of His day were a revelation of how much He cares for us as His sheep. The vines that covered the trellises of Jewish homes were symbols of the way God protects us from the heat of the day and supplies us with daily sustenance. The tilling of land opens our eyes to the wide variety of human hearts in their resistance or receptivity to the seeds of God's Word. The Gospels are full of these allusions. One writer has expressed it beautifully when she wrote, "To those who thus [through nature] acquaint themselves with Christ, the earth will nevermore be a lonely and desolate place. It will be their Father's house, filled with the presence of Him who once dwelt among men."[1]

Elizabeth Barrett Browning said the same thing in a more poetic manner when she wrote, "Earth's crammed with heaven, And every common bush afire with God; But only he who sees, takes off his shoes—The rest sit round it and pluck blackberries."[2]

Not only did Jesus create our bodies, the Bible emphasizes that He went one further step and redeemed them. "Do you not know that your body is a temple of the Holy Spirit, who is in you, whom you have received from God? You are not your own; you were bought at a price. Therefore honor God with your body" (1 Cor. 6:19-20).

Here Paul is using the language of a slave market common to his day. In choosing to act independently from God's revealed purpose for our lives, we have unwittingly sold ourselves to a cruel slave master, and our bodies suffer under his tyranny as much as the other aspects of our human nature. Jesus describes satan as, "...a murderer from the beginning, not holding to the truth, for there is no truth in him. When he lies, he speaks his native language, for he is a liar and the father of lies" (John 8:44).

The climactic demonstration of Jesus' value on our human body, however, is unquestionably the manner in which He has assumed authentic humanity Himself forever in His eternal body. He has linked Himself to humanity with a tie that will never be broken. "But our citizenship is in heaven. And we eagerly await a Savior from there, the Lord Jesus Christ, who, by the power that enables Him to bring everything under His control, will transform our lowly bodies so that they will be like His glorious body" (Phil. 3:20-21). Also, "But this man [Jesus], because He *continueth ever*, hath an unchangeable priesthood" (Heb. 7:24 KJV).

We need to avail ourselves of all the general health principles and natural remedies that God has provided for us in the Bible and His creation. "Every good and perfect gift is from above, coming down from the Father of the heavenly lights, who does not change like shifting shadows" (James 1:17).

Even before modern science had revealed the benefits of natural remedies, the Bible had emphasized the gifts of nutrition, diet, exercise, sunshine, pure air, water, and adequate sleep as healthy ways to look after our bodies. Scripture has called us to align our lives with all the counsel of God revealed in the everyday aspects of nature and living.

God has not primarily inspired the Bible as a handbook on practical ways to look after our bodies, but if we read its pages discerningly, it certainly offers very practical divine wisdom and natural remedies to care for the unique creation God brought into existence for us to live out our lives to the fullest while we are on earth.

## ENDNOTES

1.  E.G. White, *Education* (Nampa, ID: Pacific Press Publishing Association, 1952), 120.

2.  Elizabeth Barrett Browning, *Aurora Leigh* (Bk. VII 1), 812-826.

# CHAPTER SIX

# BASIC HEALTHY
# BODY NECESSITIES

# BASIC HEALTHY BODY NECESSITIES

## FOOD

Let us begin by noticing what the Bible says about food, nutrition, and diet. From the very beginning, God outlines the food He designed for Adam and Eve. "Then God said, 'Let the land produce vegetation: seed-bearing plants and trees on the land that bear fruit with seed in it, according to their various kinds.' And it was so. The land produced vegetation: plants bearing seed according to their kinds and trees bearing fruit with seed in it according to their kinds. And God saw that it was good" (Gen. 1:11-12).

When sin entered the world, God added vegetables with their remedial ability to counteract disease to human diet. "To Adam He said, 'Because you listened to your wife and ate from the tree about which I commanded you, "You must not eat of it," Cursed is the ground because of you; through painful toil you will eat of it all the days of your life. It will produce thorns and thistles for you, and you will eat the plants of the field'" (Gen. 3:17-18).

When sin entered the world, it brought with it various diseases. To counteract sickness, God added vegetables with their remedial qualities to counteract any diseases that might have entered the world.

Following the destruction of vegetable life as a result of the flood in Noah's day, God gave humans permission to eat animal flesh, but

71

in so doing He supplied some guidance to minimize the negative effects of eating flesh.

> *Then God blessed Noah and his sons, saying to them, "Be fruitful and increase in number and fill the earth. The fear and dread of you will fall upon all the beasts of the earth and all the birds of the air, upon every creature that moves along the ground, and upon all the fish of the sea; they are given into your hands. Everything that lives and moves will be food for you. Just as I gave you the green plants, I now give you everything. But you must not eat meat that has its lifeblood still in it"* (Genesis 9:1-4).

In Leviticus 11, God provided a list of flesh foods which were healthier than others to eat, and they are categorized as either clean or unclean. We misread this chapter if we take these distinctions to be purely ceremonial in nature with a purpose that enabled Jewish people to separate themselves specifically from surrounding nations. The distinctions were made long before Abraham's descendents came into existence (see Gen. 7:6-7). The animals, fishes, and birds labeled as "unclean" were universally scavengers, and God was giving the people of that day a basic rule of thumb to distinguish that which was most healthy for them to eat. What they ate was the single biggest aid to the clarity of their mind, emotions, willpower, and spirit, and hence their relationship with God.

The key text in Leviticus 11 is verse 14 where He makes diet an issue of holiness, "I am the Lord your God; consecrate yourselves and be holy, because I am holy..." (Lev. 11:44). They were to set their bodies apart to God as a way of fulfilling His divine purpose of existence for them to be a nation of priests to the rest of the nations living around them (see Exod. 19:5).

This principle is repeated over and over again throughout Scripture. Whenever God called an individual to do a special work for Him, He always commanded them to watch their diet. Samson and Daniel and Elijah are classic examples of this. In these examples, the Bible not only lists specific areas of eating and drinking to consider, it spells out the specific advantages and spiritual blessings that follow obedience to God's counsel.

*Daniel resolved not to defile himself with the royal food and wine, and he asked the chief official for permission not to defile himself this way. Now God had caused the official to show favor and sympathy to Daniel, but the official told Daniel, "I am afraid of my lord the king, who has assigned your food and drink. Why should he see you looking worse than the other young men your age? The king would then have my head because of you." Daniel then said to the guard whom the chief official had appointed over Daniel, Hananiah, Mishael and Azariah, "Please test your servants for ten days: Give us nothing but vegetables to eat and water to drink. Then compare our appearance with that of the young men who eat the royal food, and treat your servants in accordance with what you see." So he agreed to this and tested them for ten days. At the end of the ten days they looked healthier and better nourished than any of the young men who ate the royal food. So the guard took away their choice food and the wine they were to drink and gave them vegetables instead. To these four young men God gave knowledge and understanding of all kinds of literature and learning. And Daniel could understand visions and dreams of all kinds* (Daniel 1:8-17).

*John's clothes were made of camel's hair, and he had a leather belt around his waist. His food was locusts and wild honey* (Matthew 3:4).

*And the Lord spake unto Moses, saying, Speak unto the children of Israel, and say unto them, When either man or woman shall separate themselves to vow a vow of a Nazarite, to separate themselves unto the Lord: he shall separate himself from wine and strong drink, and shall drink no vinegar of wine, or vinegar of strong drink, neither shall he drink any liquor of grapes, nor eat moist grapes, or dried. All the days of his separation shall he eat nothing that is made of the vine tree, from the kernels even to the husk* (Numbers 6:1-4 KJV).

*Again the Israelites did evil in the eyes of the Lord, so the Lord delivered them into the hands of the Philistines for forty years. A certain man of Zorah, named Manoah, from the clan of the Danites, had a wife who was sterile and remained childless. The angel of the Lord appeared to her and said, "You are sterile and childless, but you are going to conceive and have a son. Now see to it that you drink no wine or other fermented drink and that you do not eat anything unclean, because you will conceive and give birth to a son. No razor may be used on his head, because the boy is to be a Nazirite, set apart to God from birth, and he will begin the deliverance of Israel from the hands of the Philistines* (Judges 13:1-5).

One of the saddest things that happened in Hebrew history was the way Jewish people eventually turned these guidelines about food and diet into a hallmark of spiritual superiority that separated them from their national neighbors. When non-Jewish people realized that their eating and living habits categorized them as personally unclean by Jews, it caused a deep alienation between them and the children of Israel. This whole issue was dealt with decisively at the first church council held in Jerusalem, and discussed in a practical way in Romans chapter 14 where the consequences of separation between Jewish Christians and Gentile Christians living together in community was hammered out. God never intended food to be a thing that separated anybody, and He lays down the crowning principle that "the kingdom of God is not a matter of eating and drinking, but of righteousness, peace and joy in the Holy Spirit, because anyone who serves Christ in this way is pleasing to God and approved by men" (Rom. 14:17-18).

*Therefore let us stop passing judgment on one another. Instead, make up your mind not to put any stumbling block or obstacle in your brother's way. As one who is in the Lord Jesus, I am fully convinced that no food is unclean in itself. But if anyone regards something as unclean, then for him it is unclean. If your brother is distressed because of what you eat, you are no longer acting in love. Do not by your eating destroy your brother for whom Christ died. Do not allow what you consider good to be spoken of as evil. For the kingdom of God is not a matter of eating and drinking, but of righteousness, peace and joy in the Holy Spirit, because anyone who serves Christ in this way is pleasing to God and approved by men. Let us therefore make every effort to do what leads to peace and to mutual edification. Do not destroy the work of God for the sake of food. All food is clean, but it is wrong for a man to eat anything that causes someone else to stumble. It is better not to eat meat or drink wine or to do anything else that will cause your brother to fall* (Romans 14: 13-21).

The distinctions of "clean" and "unclean" are laid aside in the New Testament. The new guidelines become to eat and drink those things that are the healthiest and best nurture our bodies as temples of the Holy Spirit (see 1 Cor. 6:19-20).

## EXERCISE

Exercise of our physical bodies is another natural remedy that is very important to God, "Do you not know that in a race all the runners run, but only one gets the prize? Run in such a way as to get the prize. Everyone who competes in the games goes into strict training. They do it to get a crown that will not last; but we do it to get a crown that will last forever. Therefore I do not run like a man running aimlessly; I do not fight like a man beating the air. No, I beat my body and make it my slave so that after I have preached to others, I myself will not be disqualified for the prize" (1 Cor. 9:24-27).

In the same way that diet turned into a divisive fetish, bodily exercises ultimately assumed a similar status among many Jewish people. Paul lumps the two together in order to not detract from the spiritual impact of the Gospel. To turn a blessing given by God into a means to earn merit with Him was the epitome of legalism and showed a total misunderstanding of the grace of God demonstrated to us in the life and death of Jesus. So while exercise is still important to all Christians to keep our bodies in ultimate condition, it is never to become an obsessive compulsion used as an underlying manifestation of "super-spirituality."

*You've been raised on the Message of the faith and have followed sound teaching. Now pass on this counsel to the followers of Jesus there, and you'll be a good servant of Jesus. Stay clear of silly stories that get dressed up as religion. Exercise daily in God—no spiritual flabbiness, please! Workouts in the gymnasium are useful, but a disciplined life in God is far more so, making you fit both today and forever* (1 Timothy 4:6-7 TM).

## SUNSHINE

Sunshine is another natural remedy given by God to bless our lives and healthiness. Some of the following passages from Scripture are using sunshine as a metaphor for happiness but there is no getting away from the fact that they all emphasize the positive impact of sunshine on physical health. Sunshine is especially significant to those passing through times of convalescence from sickness. It not only lifts the human soul and spirit from discouragement and self-preoccupation, it also has literal physical benefits. Some preliminary studies involving intakes of vitamin E higher than the daily-recommended requirement have shown that vitamin E may be useful in treating many skin conditions and preventing the following ailments: menstrual pain, low sperm count, inflammation of eye tissues, cataracts, restless leg syndrome, and relief from muscle cramping, Alzheimer's disease, Parkinson's disease, rheumatoid arthritis, asthma, various diabetes related complications and may be helpful in treating and preventing diabetes, cardiovascular disease, prostate cancer, and breast cancer.[1]

The following Scripture illustrates how, in His love for His people, God constantly shared with them important principles for their physical good health.

> *May the Lord bless His land with the precious dew from heaven above and with the deep waters that lie below; with the best the sun brings forth and the finest the moon can yield; with the choicest gifts of the ancient mountains and the fruitfulness of the everlasting hills; with the best gifts of the earth and its fullness and the favor of Him who dwelt in the burning bush* (Deuteronomy 33:13-16).

> *…He puts poor people on their feet again; He rekindles burned-out lives with fresh hope, restoring dignity and respect to their lives—a place in the sun! For the very structures of earth are God's; He has laid out His operations on a firm foundation…* (1 Samuel 2:8 TM).

*...Is like first light at daybreak without a cloud in the sky, like green grass carpeting earth, glistening under fresh rain...* (2 Samuel 23:4 TM).

*...For Jews it was all sunshine and laughter: they celebrated, they were honored...* (Esther 8:16 TM).

*...Your world will be washed in sunshine, every shadow dispersed by dayspring. ...He shines a spotlight into caves of darkness and hauls deepest darkness, into the noonday sun. ...Was I ever so awed by the sun's brilliance and moved by the moon's beauty...* (Job 11:17, 12:22, 31:26 TM).

*But their silence fills the earth: unspoken truth is spoken everywhere. God makes a huge dome for the sun—a superdome! The morning sun's a new husband leaping from his honeymoon bed, the daybreaking sun an athlete racing to the tape. ...Clean the slate, God, so we can start the day fresh! Keep me from stupid sins, from thinking I can take over your work; Then I can start this day sun-washed, scrubbed clean of the grime of sin...* (Psalm 19:4-5,11 TM).

*The God of gods—it's God!—speaks out, shouts, "Earth!" welcomes the sun in the east, farewells the disappearing sun in the west* (Psalm 50:1 TM).

*All sunshine and sovereign is God, generous in gifts and glory. He doesn't scrimp with his traveling companions. ...Dressed up in sunshine, and all heaven stretched out for Your tent...* (Psalm 84:11, 104:2 TM).

*Oh, how sweet the light of day, and how wonderful to live in the sunshine!...* (Ecclesiastes 11:7 TM).

*Don't look down on me because I'm dark, darkened by the sun's harsh rays. My brothers ridiculed me and sent me to work in the fields. They made me care for the face of the earth, but I had no time to care for my own face* (Song of Solomon 1:6 TM).

*...You know that as soon as the sun rises, pouring down its scorching heat, the flower withers. Its petals wilt and, before*

*you know it, that beautiful face is a barren stem. Well, that's a picture of the "prosperous life." At the very moment everyone is looking on in admiration, it fades away to nothing* (James 1:11 TM).

*...shade from the burning sun and shelter from the driving rain* (Isaiah 4:6 TM).

*...sunlight, like a whole week of sunshine at once, will flood the land* (Isaiah 30:26 TM).

*...If you are generous with the hungry and start giving yourselves to the down-and-out, your lives will begin to glow in the darkness your shadowed lives will be bathed in sunlight...* (Isaiah 58:10 TM).

*...But for you, sunrise! The sun of righteousness will dawn on those who honor My name, healing radiating from its wings. You will be bursting with energy, like colts frisky and frolicking...* (Malachi 4:2 TM).

*...This is what God does. He gives His best—the sun to warm and the rain to nourish—to everyone, regardless: the good and bad, the nice and nasty...* (Matthew 5:45 TM).

## WARMTH

Warmth is required for our physical bodies; God provides in a variety of ways for our needs as the following Scriptures describe.

*King David grew old. The years had caught up with him. Even though they piled blankets on him, he couldn't keep warm...* (1 Kings 1:1 TM).

*Have I ever left a poor family shivering in the cold when they had no warm clothes?...* (Job 31:19 TM).

*...They'll see that you take care of the poor that you take care of poor people in trouble. Provide a warm, dry place in bad weather, provide a cool place when it's hot. Brutal oppressors are like a winter blizzard...* (Isaiah 25:4 TM).

## PURE AIR

Pure air and adequate ventilation are yet another important natural remedy for the health of our bodies. This is not only especially the case for convalescents, but important for every sleeping area.

> *...Don't feel sorry for him. Clean out the pollution of wrongful murder from Israel so that you'll be able to live well and breathe clean air* (Deuteronomy 19:13 TM).

> *...every man, woman, and child would die for lack of air* (Job 34:15 TM).

> *Bilious and bloated, they gas, "God is gone." Their words are poison gas, fouling the air; they poison...* (Psalm 14:1 TM).

> *I'm hurt and in pain; give me space for healing, and mountain air* (Psalm 69:29 TM).

> *What's this I see, approaching from the desert, raising clouds of dust, filling the air with sweet smells and pungent aromatics? ...Wake up, North Wind, get moving, South Wind! Breathe on my garden, fill the air with spice fragrance...* (Song of Solomon 3:6, 4:16 TM).

> *...A new power is in operation. The Spirit of life in Christ, like a strong wind, has magnificently cleared the air, freeing you from a fated lifetime of brutal tyranny at the hands of sin and death* (Romans 8:2 TM).

> *...Go out into the world uncorrupted, a breath of fresh air in this squalid and polluted society. Provide people with a glimpse of good living and of the living God. Carry the light-giving Message into the night...* (Philippians 2:15 TM).

## WATER

The minimization of water in our lives probably affects more elements of physical health than any other single natural remedy. The human body, which is made up of between 55 and 75 percent water (lean people have more water in their bodies because muscle holds more water than fat), is in need of constant water replenishment. Our lungs expel between two and four cups of water each day through normal breathing—even more on a cold day. If your feet sweat, there goes another cup of water. If you make half a dozen trips to the bathroom during the day, that's six cups of water. If you perspire, you expel about two cups of water, which doesn't include exercise-induced perspiration.

A person would have to lose 10 percent of his or her body weight in fluids to be considered dehydrated, but as little as 2 percent can affect athletic performance, cause tiredness, and dull critical thinking abilities. Adequate water consumption can help lessen the chance of kidney stones, keep joints lubricated, prevent and lessen the severity of colds and flu, and help prevent constipation. Water is crucial to our health. It makes up, on average, 60 percent of our body weight. Every system in our body depends on water.

Lack of water can lead to dehydration, a condition that occurs when we don't have enough water in our body to carry on normal functions. Even mild dehydration—as little as a 1 percent to 2 percent loss of our body weight—can sap our energy and make us tired. Dehydration poses a particular health risk for the very young and the very old. Signs and symptoms of dehydration include excessive thirst, fatigue, headache, dry mouth, little or no urination, muscle weakness, dizziness, and light-headedness.

God talks about our need for water in the Scriptures.

*God called the dry ground "land," and the gathered waters He called "seas." And God saw that it was good (Genesis 1:10).*

*Just then God opened her (Hagar) eyes. She looked. She saw a well of water. She went to it and filled her canteen and gave the boy a long, cool drink (Genesis 21:19 TM).*

*...Nobody hungry, nobody thirsty, shade from the sun, shelter from the wind, For the Compassionate One guides them, takes them to the best springs... (Isaiah 49:10 TM).*

*Wild animals will say "Thank you!"—the coyotes and the buzzards—Because I provided water in the desert, rivers through the sun-baked earth. Drinking water for the people I chose...* (Isaiah 43:20 TM).

## SLEEP

Adequate sleep is yet another natural remedy God gives us ample counsel on to follow.

*I'll make the country a place of peace—you'll be able to go to sleep at night without fear; I'll get rid of the wild beasts; I'll eliminate war...* (Leviticus 26:6 TM).

*That night the king couldn't sleep. He ordered the record book, the day-by-day journal of events, to be brought and read to him* (Esther 6:1 TM).

*...It came in a scary dream one night, after I had fallen into a deep, deep sleep...* (Job 4:13 TM).

*...And don't think that night, when people sleep off their troubles, will bring you any relief...* (Job 36:20 TM).

*If you wake me each morning with the sound of your loving voice, I'll go to sleep each night trusting in you. Point out the road I must travel. I'm all ears, all eyes before you* (Psalm 43:7 TM).

See also Psalm 3:5, 4:8, 77:4, 127:2, 148:3.

Like every other blessing, too much sleep can become a curse when it turns into slothfulness.

*You lazy fool, look at an ant. Watch it closely; let it teach you a thing or two. Nobody has to tell it what to do. All summer it stores up food; at harvest it stockpiles provisions. So how long are you going to laze around doing nothing? How long before you get out of bed? A nap here, a nap there, a day off here, a day off there, sit back, take it easy—do you know what comes next? Life collapses on loafers; lazybones go hungry. Don't be too fond of sleep; you'll end up in the poorhouse. Wake up and get up; then there'll be food on the table. Make hay while the sun shines—that's smart; go fishing during harvest—that's stupid. Good-tempered leaders invigorate lives; they're like spring rain and sunshine* (Proverbs 6:6-11, 19:15, 10:5, 20:13, 16:15 TM).

*Over-work makes for restless sleep. Hard and honest work earns a good night's sleep, Whether supper is beans or steak. But a rich man's belly gives him insomnia* (Ecclesiastes 5:3,12 TM).

*…I can't sleep—I'm that upset, that troubled* (Isaiah 38:15 TM).

*Just then I woke up and looked around—what a pleasant and satisfying sleep!* (Jeremiah 31:26 TM)

*…They'll drink themselves falling-down drunk. Dead drunk, they'll sleep—and sleep, and sleep…and they'll never wake up…* (Jeremiah 51:39 TM).

*In the second year of his reign, King Nebuchadnezzar started having dreams that disturbed him deeply. He couldn't sleep…he said to them, "I had a dream that I can't get out of my mind. I can't sleep until I know what it means"* (Daniel 2:1-3 TM).

*When He came back to His disciples, He found them sound asleep. He said to Peter, "Can't you stick it out with Me a single hour? Stay alert; be in prayer so you don't wander into temptation without even knowing you're in danger. There is a part of you that is eager, ready for anything in God. But there's another part that's as lazy as an old dog sleeping by the fire." …So, whatever you do, don't go to sleep at the switch. Pray constantly that you will have the strength and wits to make it through everything that's coming and end up on your feet before the Son of Man. …He said, "What business do you have sleeping? Get up. Pray so you won't give in to temptation"* (Matthew 26:40; Luke 21:36, 22:46 TM).

*But make sure that you don't get so absorbed and exhausted in taking care of all your day-by-day obligations that you lose track of the time and doze off, oblivious to God…* (Romans 13:11 TM).

*...If you pull the covers back over your head and sleep on, oblivious to God, I'll return when you least expect it, break into your life like a thief in the night* (Revelation 3:2 TM).

## GUARD WELL

Guard well how you use the physical members of your body. It is the only thing you have to express your inner values, your love, and loyalties for God. The parts of your body are the only means you have to physically express righteousness in your behavior for God's glory or unrighteousness that not only brings disrepute on your Creator and Redeemer but also your own moral nature and interpersonal relationships and reputation.

> *In the same way, count yourselves dead to sin but alive to God in Christ Jesus. Therefore do not let sin reign in your mortal body so that you obey its evil desires. Do not offer the parts of your body to sin, as instruments of wickedness, but rather offer yourselves to God, as those who have been brought from death to life; and offer the parts of your body to Him as instruments of righteousness. For sin shall not be your master, because you are not under law, but under grace* (Romans 6:11-14).

Jesus' counsel to the disciples in Gethsemane suggests that satan can surround us with circumstances that make us tired and block our mental and spiritual discernment. We need to be alert to what is going on around us so that any resulting impact on the condition of our bodies does not hinder our relationship with God. (See Mark 14:37-38.)

## ENDNOTE

1. Linus Pauling Institute, Micronutrient Research for Optimum Health. See http://lpi.oregonstate.edu; accessed December 5, 2009.

# CHAPTER SEVEN

# BASIC GUIDELINES
# FOR A HEALTHY BODY

# BASIC GUIDELINES
# FOR A HEALTHY BODY

Richard Foster has written much about the benefit of the spiritual disciplines that God has encouraged us to pursue in our Christian lives.[1] Before we encounter a personal relationship with Jesus, there is a quality in our natural humanity that is undisciplined and gravitates toward destructive habits of life.

> *When tempted, no one should say, "God is tempting me." For God cannot be tempted by evil, nor does he tempt anyone; but each one is tempted when, by his own evil desire, he is dragged away and enticed. Then, after desire has conceived, it gives birth to sin; and sin, when it is full-grown, gives birth to death* (James 1:13-15).

The Bible has shared much about habits that need to be intentionally cultivated in order to unconsciously counteract these tendencies and propensities in our human nature in such a way that they become just as natural as the old habits used to be.

> *His divine power has given us everything we need for life and godliness through our knowledge of Him who called us by His own glory and goodness. Through these He has given us His very great and precious promises, so that through them you may participate in the divine nature and escape the corruption in the world caused by evil desires. For this very reason, make every effort to add to your faith goodness; and to goodness, knowledge; and to knowledge, self-control; and to self-control, perseverance; and to perseverance, godliness; and to godliness,*

*brotherly kindness; and to brotherly kindness, love. For if you possess these qualities in increasing measure, they will keep you from being ineffective and unproductive in your knowledge of our Lord Jesus Christ. But if anyone does not have them, he is nearsighted and blind, and has forgotten that he has been cleansed from his past sins. Therefore, my brothers, be all the more eager to make your calling and election sure. For if you do these things, you will never fall, and you will receive a rich welcome into the eternal kingdom of our Lord and Savior Jesus Christ* (2 Peter 1:3-11).

*As for you, you were dead in your transgressions and sins, in which you used to live when you followed the ways of this world and of the ruler of the kingdom of the air, the spirit who is now at work in those who are disobedient. All of us also lived among them at one time, gratifying the cravings of our sinful nature and following its desires and thoughts. Like the rest, we were by nature objects of wrath. But because of his great love for us, God, who is rich in mercy, made us alive with Christ even when we were dead in transgressions—it is by grace you have been saved. And God raised us up with Christ and seated us with Him in the heavenly realms in Christ Jesus, in order that in the coming ages He might show the incomparable riches of His grace, expressed in his kindness to us in Christ Jesus. For it is by grace you have been saved, through faith—and this not from yourselves, it is the gift of God—not by works, so that no one can boast. For we are God's workmanship, created in Christ Jesus to do good works, which God prepared in advance for us to do* (Ephesians 2:1-10).

*But the fruit of the Spirit is love, joy, peace, patience, kindness, goodness, faithfulness, gentleness and self-control. Against such things there is no law. Those who belong to Christ Jesus have crucified the sinful nature with its passions and desires. Since we live by the Spirit, let us keep in step with the Spirit. Let us not become conceited, provoking and envying each other* (Galatians 5:22-26).

Cultivate a positive bond between the body and the mind. Whatever we focus our minds on eventually determines the direction of our lives.

*For as he thinketh in his heart, so is he... (Proverbs 23:7 KJV).*

*Finally, brothers, whatever is true, whatever is noble, whatever is right, whatever is pure, whatever is lovely, whatever is admirable—if anything is excellent or praiseworthy—think about such things (Philippians 4:8).*

Cultivate a positive bond between the body and the spirit.

*A merry heart maketh a cheerful countenance: but by sorrow of the heart the spirit is broken. The heart of him that hath understanding seeketh knowledge: but the mouth of fools feedeth on foolishness. All the days of the afflicted are evil: but he that is of a merry heart hath a continual feast (Proverbs 15:13-15 KJV).*

The body is a powerful gift to express and develop harmony in every marriage relationship.

*For this reason a man will leave his father and mother and be united to his wife, and they will become one flesh. The man and his wife were both naked, and they felt no shame (Genesis 2:24-25).*

*Enjoy life with your wife, whom you love, all the days of this meaningless life that God has given you under the sun... (Ecclesiastes 9:9).*

*Come away, my lover, and be like a gazelle or like a young stag on the spice-laden mountains (Song of Solomon 8:14).*

*...since there is so much immorality, each man should have his own wife, and each woman her own husband. The husband should fulfill his marital duty to his wife, and likewise the wife to her husband. The wife's body does not belong to her alone but also to her husband. In the same way, the husband's body does not belong to him alone but also to his wife. Do not deprive each other except by mutual consent and for a time, so that you may*

*devote yourselves to prayer. Then come together again so that Satan will not tempt you because of your lack of self-control. I say this as a concession, not as a command. I wish that all men were as I am. But each man has his own gift from God; one has this gift, another has that* (1 Corinthians 7:2-7).

Constantly guard against demonic intrusions into your body. Be trained in the elements of spiritual warfare (protection). Learn to fast in issues of temptation and destructive desires.

*Jesus, full of the Holy Spirit, returned from the Jordan and was led by the Spirit in the desert, where for forty days He was tempted by the devil. He ate nothing during those days, and at the end of them He was hungry. The devil said to Him, "If you are the Son of God, tell this stone to become bread." Jesus answered, "It is written: 'Man does not live on bread alone'"* (Luke 4:1-4).

*But when you fast, put oil on your head and wash your face, so that it will not be obvious to men that you are fasting, but only to your Father, who is unseen; and your Father, who sees what is done in secret, will reward you* (Matthew 6:17-18).

Live in the present existence of the Kingdom of God (prayer/sickness/healing).

*After John was put in prison, Jesus went into Galilee, proclaiming the good news of God. "The time has come," He said. "The kingdom of God is near. Repent and believe the good news!" As Jesus walked beside the Sea of Galilee, He saw Simon and his brother Andrew casting a net into the lake, for they were fishermen. "Come, follow me," Jesus said, "and I will make you fishers of men." At once they left their nets and followed Him* (Mark 1:14-18).

*One day Peter and John were going up to the temple at the time of prayer—at three in the afternoon. Now a man crippled from birth was being carried to the temple gate called Beautiful, where he was put every day to beg from those going into the temple courts. When he saw Peter and John about to enter, he asked them for money. Peter looked straight at him, as did John.*

*Then Peter said, "Look at us!" So the man gave them his atten-*
*tion, expecting to get something from them. Then Peter said,*
*"Silver or gold I do not have, but what I have I give you. In the*
*name of Jesus Christ of Nazareth, walk." Taking him by the*
*right hand, he helped him up, and instantly the man's feet and*
*ankles became strong. He jumped to his feet and began to walk.*
*Then he went with them into the temple courts, walking and*
*jumping, and praising God. When all the people saw him walk-*
*ing and praising God, they recognized him as the same man who*
*used to sit begging at the temple gate called Beautiful, and they*
*were filled with wonder and amazement at what had happened*
*to him* (Acts 3:1-10).

Avail yourselves of the God given role of Christian community. None of us were created to be loners. While it is true that we must each individually enter into a personal relationship with God, the New Testament has a very strong emphasis on living in community. We are called to be, the "people of God" who have become what God longed for initially in establishing the nation of Israel. All the passages in the Old Testament applying to national Israel are transferred to the Christian Church in the New Testament (see Rom. 2:28-29; Gal. 3:26-29; 1 Pet. 2:9-10). Such a relationship with each other is a safeguard for spiritual support and accountability.

## ENDNOTE

1. Richard Foster, *The Celebration of Discipline* (London, UK: Hodder & Stoughton, 1984).

# CHAPTER EIGHT

# THE HUMAN SOUL

# THE HUMAN SOUL

*...May your whole...soul...be kept blameless at the coming of our Lord Jesus Christ* (1 Thessalonians 5:23).

## THE NATURE OF THE HUMAN SOUL

The Greek word in the New Testament in First Thessalonians 5:23 translated as "soul" is *psuche*[1] and the English rendition of this is "psyche." It represents the part of our nature that is characteristically human and embraces all things understood as comprising the psyche. It includes thinking processes, emotional responses, and behavioral choices. It is the Hebrew equivalent of *nephesh* used in Genesis 2:7: "...the Lord God formed the man from the dust of the ground and breathed into his nostrils the breath of life, and the man became *a living being.*" The King James Version renders this expression as "...and man became a living soul," but this is open to misunderstanding. The Hebrew language makes it clear that humans don't "have" a soul; rather they "are" a soul. We capture the true meaning of the word when we say of an aged friend, "She's a dear old soul!" And by that we mean the person in her totality.

Some traditions have seen the soul as synonymous with the Greek use of "immortal spirit," but there is no biblical evidence for this. Old Testament uses of *nephesh* include breath (see Job 41:21), life (see 1 Kings 17:21; 2 Sam. 18:13), heart as the seat of affection

95

(see Gen. 34:3; Song of Sol. 1:7), or as a personal pronoun emphasis (see Ps. 3:2). The nephesh is made by God (see Jer. 38:16), can die (see Judg. 16:30), be eaten (see Num. 31:19), be killed (see Ezek. 22:25), be redeemed (see Ps. 34:22) and refreshed (see Ps. 19:7). While it describes the total nature of a living person, it has no existence apart from the body. It never leaves the person to pursue an independent life of its own and is not identical with the vital life-force of the person. The departure of the soul is actually a metaphor for death. The living soul dies when breath leaves the body.

The Old Testament also uses *nephesh* to describe specific feelings such as grief (see 1 Sam. 1:15), impatience (see Exod. 6:9), fornication (see Hos. 4:12), falsehood (see Mic. 2:11), jealousy (see Num. 5:14), and sleep (see Isa. 29:10), that people express as part of their total humanity. In so doing, nephesh comes close to the classic understanding of the psyche.

In the New Testament, the Greek word *psuche* has more nuances and variations. Like *nephesh,* it is a term for the whole person (see Acts 3:23, 2:41, 7:14, 27:37; Matt. 11:29), but its primary use depicts the natural physical life of humans (see Matt. 10:39; Luke 17:33; John 12:25). It is more than just being physically alive, however. The soul is that aspect of humanity in which the human self expresses itself. Moreover, it has overt religious connotations. It is life lived in the full sense that God intended it in His service and praise. It is to be pastorally nurtured and implies responsibility. It is the self of man that is lived before God and has to give account. As such, humans can lose their soul, or save it, an outcome that will only be revealed at the last judgment.

Jesus told several stories to bring home to His hearers the importance of this understanding. On one occasion, He told them this parable:

> *The ground of a certain rich man produced a good crop. He thought to himself, "What shall I do? I have no place to store my crops." Then he said, "This is what I'll do. I will tear down my barns and build bigger ones, and there I will store all my grain and my goods. And I'll say to myself, 'You have plenty of*

*good things laid up for many years. Take life easy; eat, drink and be merry.'" But God said to him, "You fool! This very night your life [soul] will be demanded from you. Then who will get what you have prepared for yourself?" This is how it will be with anyone who stores up things for himself but is not rich toward God* (Luke 12:16-21).

To be rich toward God is to freely make Him our greatest priority in all aspects of life— intellectually, emotionally, spiritually, bodily, and materially.

On another occasion, Jesus called the crowd to Him along with His disciples and said:

*If anyone would come after Me, he must deny himself and take up his cross and follow Me. For whoever wants to save his life [soul] will lose it, but whoever loses his life [soul] for Me and for the gospel will save it. What good is it for a man to gain the whole world, yet forfeit his soul? Or what can a man give in exchange for his soul? If anyone is ashamed of Me and My words in this adulterous and sinful generation, the Son of Man will be ashamed of him when He comes in his Father's glory with the holy angels* (Mark 8:34-38).

"Do not be afraid of those who kill the body but cannot kill the soul." Jesus says. "Rather, be afraid of the One who can destroy both soul and body in hell" (Matt. 10:28). By this He was referring to the time when every person has to face God in the judgment.

As such, it becomes clear that the term *soul* is a description for psychological life in our modern use of the term "psyche," especially as it is lived out before God. It is the place of feelings (see Acts 15:24), can be influenced by others (see Matt. 12:18), has to choose (see Acts 14:2; Matt. 12:18), and can experience joy, sorrow, and love (see Mark 14:34, 12:30; Luke 2:35).

There is a sense in which the soul of a Christian will survive after death (see Luke 12:4, 20, 21:19; 2 Peter 6:9), but only following the resurrection of the body at the Second Coming of Jesus. In itself, however, it is not inherently immortal or detached from the body in any way. As such, it has no intermediate state apart from life in the human body. Its existence will reach its goal only after death.

## THE SOUL AND THE IMAGE OF GOD

It has already been mentioned that relationships are one of the two primary concepts undergirding the meaning of the term *the image of God* mentioned in Genesis 1:26-27. In creating humanity as male and female, God has included a unique dynamic in the way the human soul functions. The relationships between men and women assume a vital part of the soul's activity in each person. Various cultures socialize the way men and women express their psyches differently. The Book of Genesis hints that women are primarily relationship-oriented in their psyche (see Gen. 3:16), while men are primarily task-oriented (see Gen. 3:19).

The other primary concept foundational in humanity's reflection of the image of God that we have discussed was how Adam and Eve were given representative rulership over the creation entrusted to them. It is inevitable that this issue will also profoundly affect how the human soul functions. Men and women can abuse the responsibility of caring for the planet we live on through self-centered motives of personal gain, or they can live lives of sensitive and responsible ownership. How the soul chooses to deal with the reality of personal sinfulness determines the outcome.

## THE IMPACT OF SIN ON THE SOUL

Sin has had a dramatic impact on the human soul as well as the body. It was pointed out previously that thinking patterns became defensive and irrational. The man blamed his wife and, indirectly, God as well for what had happened (see Gen. 3:12), and the woman disowned any personal responsibility for her choices (see Gen. 3:13). They both experienced the emotions of shame and fear for the first time (see Gen. 3:7,9). Their behavioral choices ceased to flow out of a trust and love of their Creator and sprang out of shame, defensiveness, and self-centered independence. They sought to cover their nakedness in their own way and tried to hide from God (see

Gen. 3:7-8). It became evident that the human will had become impotent to do what it was designed to do. The design had been sabotaged and as a result made choices that should never have been made.

By the time of Noah, the record says that, "...God saw that the wickedness of man was great in the earth, and that *every* imagination of the thoughts of his heart was only evil continually" (Gen. 6:5 KJV). Humanity had become so depraved that all aspects of the "image of God" had well nigh been obliterated. "Every" imagination of the thoughts of his heart was only evil continually. The prophet, Jeremiah, reinforces this tragic condition when he says, "The heart is deceitful above all things and beyond cure. Who can understand it?" (Jer. 17:9). This suggests strongly that it is impossible for the human will of itself to choose to do anything that is not intrinsically self-centered and thus, in some way, also ultimately evil.

Down through history, theologians have repeatedly struggled with this question. The earliest historically preserved debate occurred between Pelagius (ca. A.D. 354-440) and Augustine (A.D. 354-430). Pelagius was an ascetic monk and reformer who denied the doctrine of original sin from Adam and was declared a heretic by the early Church. While in Rome, he had become concerned about the moral laxity of society. He blamed this laxity on the theology of divine grace preached by Augustine, among others. It seemed to him that Augustine was teaching a doctrine contrary to traditional Christian understandings of grace and free will, by turning humanity, into a mere automaton. Augustine, however, had come from an early life of immorality, and his theology reflected the impotence of his own will in the struggle he had experienced in endeavors to overcome these issues.

The same debate surfaced again strongly between Martin Luther (1483-1546) and Desiderius Erasmus (1466-1536) during the time of the Protestant Reformation. In 1525 Luther published his major work, "Concerning Bound Choice," as a response to Erasmus' earlier presentation, "On Free Will." At issue was whether human beings, after the Fall of Man, are free to choose good or evil. Luther maintained that sin incapacitates human beings from working out their own salvation, and as a result they are completely unable to bring themselves to God. God must therefore take the initiative, and when He does so, He redeems the entire person, including the will, which is liberated to serve God. Most of the Protestant reformers, and notably John Calvin (1509-1564), embraced this belief as a reaction against the abuses of the medieval church and its erroneous belief that the human will was totally able to earn merit in God's eyes. The performance of good works as a payment for sins and the payment of money to lessen God's punishment to relatives who had lived sinful lives and had died, were two of the main abuses of the human will that prompted outrage in Protestant circles.

Calvin rigorously taught that the human will was totally in bondage to sin and incapable of making right choices unless God arbitrarily predetermined it beforehand. Calvin had a strong influence on the Puritans, many of whom migrated to the Americas to escape persecution from the medieval church at the time. Any doctrine emphasizing the bondage of the will and free choice soon languished in a new land where exercise of the will became the foundation of ultimate prosperity. Humanity could do anything—from conquering the wild west to ultimately putting a man on the moon.

When John Wesley (1703-1791) visited America, he articulated a theology that soon captured the ethos of an emerging nation. The United Methodist Book of Discipline (2004) calls this theology "prevenient grace," and defines it as, "...the divine love that surrounds all humanity and precedes any and all of our conscious impulses. This grace prompts our first wish to please God, our first glimmer of understanding concerning God's will, and our 'first slight transient conviction' of having sinned against God. God's grace also awakens in us an earnest longing for deliverance from sin and death and moves us toward repentance and faith."[2] Wesley rejected the total bondage of the will and maintained that human choice had a real role to play in a Christian's personal growth. It exists prior to and without reference to anything humans may have done. As humans are corrupted by the effects of sin, prevenient grace allows persons to engage their God-given free will to choose the salvation offered by God in Jesus Christ—or to reject that offer.

Jesus often asked people who approached Him for help, "What do you want of me?" (see Mark 10:51; John 1:38). In so doing, He was asking them to articulate their desires. They were expressing the choices they wanted to make but could not because of their situation. In every case, Jesus bestowed on those who asked for healing the ability to freely exercise a will that, up until then, they had been unable to do. Addressing a paralyzed man, He said, "I tell you, get up, take your mat and go home. Immediately he stood up in front of them, took what he had been lying on and went home praising God" (Luke 5:24-25). If the man had said, "I can't!" then he would have remained as he was.

The ultimate bondage of the human will is witnessed in demonic possession. Repeatedly, Jesus delivered men and women from this condition and liberated them to choose to follow Him (see Luke 8:38-39, 5:27). It is comparable to a small child calling out to his father because he wants to write his name on a piece of paper but is unable to do so. The father lovingly comes and puts his strong hand over the child's weak hand and not only strengthens it but guides it to write as the boy had longed inwardly to do, but could not on his own.

## FAMILY OF ORIGIN INFLUENCE

As a baby develops psychologically, socially, and spiritually into an adult human being, the major formative influences are inevitably its family of origin or other significant support systems. During those times and experiences, the dynamics each child encounters are extremely complex and widely variant, dependent on his or her individual circumstances. There are many different stages to traverse in learning development, psycho-social development, moral development, and faith development.

Harville Hendrix has outlined how children are wounded in the development of their psychological and social journey in life when they experience a deficit in specific aspects of nurture they need to receive from their support system in any developmental stage. When that happens, a child unconsciously chooses one of two approaches to the need they have not received from their parents. They decide to either pursue what they have missed out on (maximizing behavior) or they assume that they will never receive what they missed out on and choose to give up trying to receive it (minimizing behavior).[3]

Because of their own psychological wounding, it is impossible for parents to avoid wounding the souls of their children as they grow up. Even if parents do their very best to provide a healthy and safe environment for their children, the children usually misinterpret the parents' actions and motives as they pass through their normal developmental stages. So that they can function in the world as they experience it, and protect themselves from real or perceived dangers to their emotional and physical safety and identity, every child adopts a self-chosen strategy in order to survive. As a child, those strategies are absolutely necessary for survival, but as he or she grows into adulthood, those same chosen strategies that had earlier helped them cope with life, have become deeply ingrained over time, and prove to be counter-productive. Thought patterns and life scripts that have been adopted and thoroughly reinforced over time have become entrenched habit patterns that are hard to dislodge or change, and often lead to a measure of dysfunction in their families and future relationships.

The Enneagram is another system of exploring the human soul on the same basis. The uniqueness of this approach is the way it moves toward wholeness and healing by first of all unveiling a person's hidden but basic defensive strategy developed in childhood for security and meaningful existence. This unveiling can be a very painful and confronting experience in adulthood. The strategy, termed a "compulsion," is aimed at protecting, attaining, and maintaining the goal of personal fulfilment. It was originally chosen in childhood because the world was experienced as alienating. In view of this felt alienation, a choice was made about how to save oneself by choosing a certain way to be a person. Unfortunately, this actually constituted a limitation of true human essence modeled by Jesus in His humanity.[4]

Both these approaches reveal not only an intimate awareness of how family of origin dynamics impact all of us, but how each of us can eventually choose to take ownership of our lives rather than remaining prisoners. In so doing, we can move beyond, and live above, any negative circumstances that may have impacted us in childhood. Those deeply ingrained habit patterns of thinking will never be totally eradicated from our lives, but an awareness of their presence and functions gives us the opportunity to transcend them whenever they surface.

Although the Bible is not written as a text book on psychology, several Christian authors have traced these sorts of dynamics in the lives of prominent men and women in the Bible. John Sanford has given us much insight into the lives of Jacob, Joseph, and Moses by examining their families of origin and analyzing each personal journey toward becoming an individual, separate from their father, mother, and childhood circumstances.[5] The favoritism of Isaac to his eldest son Esau and of his wife Rebecca to their youngest son Jacob, is a classic example of the influence of dysfunctional oedipal triangles.

Earl Henslin has also explored the classical dysfunction seen in King David's upbringing and the later effects it had on his own family. He investigates the effect of David's style of fathering on Solomon's life and the co-dependency manifested in Abigail's relationship to her husband.[6]

We must never assume that the experiences of human beings recorded in Scripture are dissimilar to ours. The enemy tries to sell us a list of common lies that we unconsciously adopt at various times in life in order to cope with difficult times. They are defense mechanisms we internalize in order to survive, but they always prove destructive for us eventually. Satan constantly seeks to sell us lies such as these about ourselves, and for that reason is called the "accuser" (see Rev. 12:10; Zech. 3:1-2). They are not, however, the truth about us. God has not "…given us the spirit of fear; but of power, and of love, and of a sound mind" (2 Tim. 1:7 KJV). Our true identity is found by looking at the identity of Christ. That identity is offered to us to possess as our own. It is how He as our Savior regards us as being now, and it is an inheritance we can inherit now. Appendix A contains a list of the truths about every Christian. Part of healing the wounds of our souls is to vigorously dispute any erroneous scripts we have bought into and replace them with the truth of who we really are.

## JESUS' SOUL

There is no evidence in Scripture that at any time in Jesus' life, His thinking patterns, emotional responses, and behavioral responses were ever dysfunctional or outside the range of true humanity as originally created by God. We have already noticed that in His childhood Jesus was "filled with wisdom, and the grace of God was upon Him...and grew in wisdom and stature, and in favor with God and men" (Luke 2:40,52). This is a metaphorical way of saying that He was psychologically healthy, despite the jibes He would have received from the people who lived in Nazareth. His sensitivity to all of sin's consequences would have been extremely painful considering the nature of His sinlessness and holiness, but it never pushed Him into any pathology.

As Jesus began His ministry, the breadth of His mind was staggering. We have noted His ability to memorize the Old Testament and correct relevant passages of Scripture when they had been misquoted by His detractors (see Matt. 19:4; Mark 12:24). His wisdom became so proverbial that eventually no teacher of the law would contest Him in debate (see Mark 2:8). He read the minds and hearts of all gathered in His presence (see Matt. 27:46). There were no destructive scripts that He had internalized from His family of origin or lies about Himself or others that satan constantly tries to sell to humanity (see John 1:14). He was not blighted by negative patterns of thinking and always sought to bring out the best in people (see John 21:15-19).

In the record of Jesus' adult life, there are examples given of a full spectrum of human emotions. At times He expressed deep anger at the spiritual abuse generated by religious leaders who should have known better (see Matt. 21:12, 23:1-39). At other times, He manifested touching compassion for troubled humanity (see Matt. 9:36). His tenderness with and encouragement for disadvantaged women and children was striking (see Matt. 10:13-16; John 8:1-11). His deep sadness for those suffering grief caused Him to shed tears (see John 11:33-35). In the great crisis of Gethsemane, He sought the companionship of His closest disciples and plead with His Father for a way out of what lay ahead (see Mark 14:32-42). During the crucifixion He cried out in agony from a sense of abandonment from His Father. There were no outbursts of an ego out of control or displays of an empty love tank seeking expressions of co-dependent fulfillment. He was always secure in His identity and never suffered from personality disorders.

In His behavioral choices, Jesus always acted out of love for sinners. He never manifested addictions characteristic of psychologically damaged humans seeking an anaesthetic from the emotional pain inflicted on their lives. He was not a workaholic. He knew how to take needed rest (see Mark 6:31) and only did those things His Father indicated (see John 14:31). He practiced spiritual disciplines to keep in touch with His Father (see Mark 1:35).

All these various expressions of His soul were consistent with absolute righteousness.

## THE COMING KINGDOM OF GOD AND THE SOUL

It has been emphasized that the central theme of Jesus' teaching was that with His coming, the Kingdom of God had burst into the world. "…Jesus went into Galilee, proclaiming the good news of God. 'The time has come,' He said. 'The kingdom of God is *near*. Repent and believe the good news!'" (Mark 1:14-15). By using the word *near*, Jesus meant "had arrived" or "was among you."

The Kingdom of God was an expression grounded in the prophetic books of the Old Testament, especially the Book of Daniel. Daniel contains a chain of four prophecies, each going over the same ground, but each giving greater detail than the one preceding it. The foundational outline upon which all the others were built is given in Daniel chapter 2 and reveals a basic outline of world history. Four dominant earthly kingdoms are described as succeeding each other, climaxing in the advent of the Kingdom of God as the fourth kingdom disintegrates (see Dan. 2:24-47, 7:15-27, 8:18-25, 9:24-27, 11:36–12:3).

The Jewish nation regarded these prophecies as pointing to the coming Messiah. They divided history into two ages, the "present age" and the "age to come" (see Eph. 1:21). The present age was characterized by all the things common to life as they knew it, such as sin, war, sickness, and death. They believed that when the Messiah came He would immediately usher in the Kingdom of God and replace life with the opposite of all the characteristics of their present age—righteousness, peace, health, and life.

The four Gospels, with their separate accounts of the ministry of Jesus, make it clear that He manifested all the elements of the anticipated age to come, the Kingdom of God. In the person of Jesus, humankind saw perfect righteousness (see John 8:46; Rom. 3:21). He spoke peace into raging storms and the turmoil of human hearts (see Mark 4:39; John 14:27). Whole villages were left without a single sick person as He passed through (see Luke 4:40). Whenever He spoke to the dead, they immediately came to life again (see Luke 7:11-15; Mark 5:35-43; John 11:38-44). Demonically possessed, insane people were restored by Jesus to their right minds (see Mark 5:15).

In the person of Jesus, the Kingdom of God had indeed come. And that involves a total reorientation of the soul's focus, as well as that of the body. God wants us to center our soul on the reality of the presence of the Kingdom of God.

What becomes clear, however, is that instead of Jesus instantly and "totally" superseding the old age and immediately replacing it with the Kingdom of God, the two ages actually overlap for a period of history. Christians still have to live in the present age with all its negative and destructive qualities. They still sin, although not willingly. They still get sick. They still experience wars and inner turmoil. And unless the Lord comes in their lifetime, they will still experience death.

The distinguishing mark of Christianity, however, is that by faith in Jesus and through the Holy Spirit living within them, the followers of Jesus can experience the realities of the Kingdom of God in a limited way in the present moment.[7] God gives them an experiential down-payment of life in the Kingdom of Heaven, which will be fully appropriated at the final consummation of all things (see Eph. 1:13-14, 6:4-5; John 3:16).

At the second coming of Jesus, the present age will be terminated forever, and what Christians have taken by faith until then will be seen to be real, just as real as it has been since the first coming of Jesus and will continue to be for the rest of eternity (see Rev. 21:1-4). In the waiting time, however, Jesus progressively transforms our human minds to think like His as we persevere in our intimacy with Him through study of His Word, obedience to His will, and openness to the indwelling Holy Spirit (see Rom. 12:1-2; 1 Cor. 2:16).

## THE IMPACT OF THE SOUL ON THE BODY AND THE SPIRIT

We need to be continually reminded that the three aspects of our humanity do not function independently of each other. The health of the soul has a profound impact on both the body and the spirit and vice versa. The Bible endorses this truth when it says, "A cheerful heart is good medicine, but a crushed spirit dries up the bones" (Prov. 17:22). "A happy heart makes the face cheerful, but heartache crushes the spirit...All the days of the oppressed are wretched, but the cheerful heart has a continual feast" (Prov. 15:13,15).

Somatic and spiritual indicators are increasingly becoming part of psychological diagnosis. Many diseases that people suffer are the result of depression, grief, anxiety, discontent, remorse, guilt, and distrust. All these tend to break down life forces and invite decay and death. On the other hand, courage, hope, faith, sympathy, and love promote health and prolong life. A contented mind and a cheerful spirit give a healthy boost to the body and strengthen the soul.

The stresses of modern living, economic strain, and crises in domestic relationships eat into the very souls of many and weaken their hold on life itself. Often a sense of guilt and remorse for sin undermines health and unbalances the mind. There is only one source for valid peace to the soul. Jesus gave an invitation to all who were weighed down and discouraged by overwhelming aspects of life. "Are you tired? Worn out? Burned out on religion? Come to me.

Get away with me and you'll recover your life. I'll show you how to take a real rest. Walk with me and work with me—watch how I do it. Learn the unforced rhythms of grace. I won't lay anything heavy or ill-fitting on you. Keep company with me and you'll learn to live freely and lightly" (Matt. 11:28-30 TM).

Nothing tends to promote health of the body and soul more than a spirit of gratitude and praise. The promises and statements of Scripture are not empty words. To read them, verbalize them, and often claim them personally for ourselves is a very effective way to resist melancholy and discouragement. It is evident from reading the Gospels that Jesus had memorized the whole of the Old Testament. He often illustrated and modeled for us the wisdom of bringing to mind verses of Scripture that the Holy Spirit anointed for unique circumstances He encountered. We would do well to follow His example for the healing of wounds inflicted in various ways on our souls. He encourages us with words such as, "Sanctify them by the truth; your word is truth" (John 17:17) and, "The Spirit gives life; the flesh counts for nothing. The words I have spoken to you are spirit and they are life" (John 6:63).

The Word of God cannot be effective in our lives without the life-giving work of the Holy Spirit. The Spirit supplies and applies His creative energy to the recorded words of Christ in the Gospels and the rest of Scripture. Seeking to understand life without this divine help severely limits our minds from understanding or perceiving true reality as it exists in the light of eternity. The second chapter of First Corinthians highlights the inability of the natural mind to understand the things of God. It is the Spirit of God alone that gives us the "mind of Christ" and His perspective on human living (see 1 Cor. 2:6-16). His mind has only health and healing as an aim for our minds.

To think like He thinks and view life as He perceives it is our only pathway to a healthy soul. It is this alone that enables us to see and combat the destructive influences of life lived without God and His divine perspective. We are admonished to "...not conform any longer to the pattern of this world, but be transformed by the renewing of your mind. Then you will be able to test and approve what God's will is—His good, pleasing and perfect will" (Rom. 12:2). This verse clarifies the reality that the healing of our souls is a gradual process of transformation that continues throughout life, rather than an instantaneous thing that happens at conversion. It is therefore imperative that we discipline our minds to focus continually on God's values in order to facilitate this ongoing healing. "...Whatever is true, whatever is noble, whatever is right, whatever is pure, whatever is lovely, whatever is admirable—if anything is excellent or praiseworthy—think about such things" (Phil. 4:8).

## ENDNOTES

1.  Gerhard Kittel and Gerhard Friedrich, eds., *Theological Dictionary of the New Testament Volume 9* (Grand Rapids, MI: Eerdmans Publishing Company, 1974), 608-660.

2.  *The Book of Discipline of the United Methodist Church* (Nashville, TN: The United Methodist Publishing House, 2004).

3.  H. Hendrix, *Keeping the Love You Find* (New York, NY: Pocket Books, 1992).

4.  Maria Beesing, Robert J. Nogosek, Patrick H. O'Leary, *The Enneagram* (Denville, NJ: Dimension Books, 2006), 124.

5.  J.A. Sanford, J.A., *The Man Who Wrestled with God* (New York, NY: Paulist Press, 1987).

6.  E.R. Henslin, *Forgiven and Free* (Nashville, TN: Thomas Nelson, 1978).

7.  George Eldon Ladd, *The Presence of the Future* (Grand Rapids, MI: Eerdmans Publishing Company, 1974).

# CHAPTER NINE

# THE HUMAN SPIRIT

# THE HUMAN SPIRIT

*May your whole spirit...be kept blameless at the coming of our Lord Jesus Christ* (1 Thessalonians 5:23).

## THE NATURE OF THE HUMAN SPIRIT

The word translated as "spirit" in the New Testament is *pneuma*. When used as an aspect of human nature, it is almost exclusively focusing on the spiritual or psychical functions of people. There are occasions where it simply denotes a human being as a whole, but always there is a strong emphasis on the spiritual aspects of that person that are God-given and enables him or her to interface with Him.[1]

## THE IMAGE OF GOD AND THE HUMAN SPIRIT

Let us return once more to the passage of Scripture in Genesis 1:26-27 for a moment. "Then God said, 'Let us make man in our image, in our likeness, and let them rule over the fish of the sea and the birds of the air, over the livestock, over all the earth, and over all the creatures that move along the ground.' So God created man in His own image, in the image of God he created him; male and female he created them."

We have already canvassed the breadth of possible meanings given to the phase *the image of God*. Central to our focus on this issue

113

of the human spirit is the response of Jesus to the Samaritan woman by the well at Sychar. Following a discussion on the different under-standing of worship between Samaritans and Jews, Jesus said, "…a time is coming and has now come when the true worshipers will worship the Father in spirit and truth, for they are the kind of wor-shipers the Father seeks. God is spirit, and His worshipers must worship in spirit and in truth" (John 4:23-24).

Jesus was announcing that when it came to worship, what was going on in the inner heart of people was God's primary interest and requirement rather than places or structures. He is looking to see if worship comes from within our innermost being and is cen-tered on Him. Although our minds and emotions and choices are definitely involved in worship, God still does not want the soul to be the fountain of worship, to be merely intellectual Christians, or emotional Christians, or behavioral Christians. He wants us to be spiritual Christians. By that, God means He desires worshipers to function first and foremost on the realm of the Holy Spirit. As a result of that focus, all aspects of their souls will automatically be brought under submission to the Spirit.

From this understanding it is evident that the human *spirit* is that aspect of our human *nature* that can connect with God as Spirit. It would include things such as worship, conscience, and intuition. But the Bible points out that before this is at all possible, God must first exercise His sovereign initiative to enable our human spirits to do so. To worship God in spirit and truth is not to try and worship Him merely out of an awareness stemming from our own unconverted human spirit. There are multitudes of ways the human spirit seeks to worship without first allowing the Holy Spirit to bring it alive to the things of God. The only worship that matters to God is to wor-ship in the sphere of God and no longer in satan's sphere, the realm of mere appearance.

In the creation account of Genesis 2:7, Jesus is described as bend-ing over the inanimate body He had just fashioned from the "dust of the earth" and breathing into Adam's nostrils the "breath of life." The Hebrew word for this is *neshamah* and implies the life-giving princi-ple from the source of all life. Genesis 1:2 describes the Spirit of God as hovering over the primeval waters. The Hebrew word here for Spirit is *ruach,* and in harmony with scriptural usage, the Spirit of God is the Holy Spirit, the third person of the Godhead. From this place onward, throughout the whole Scripture, the Spirit of God is portrayed as the divine agent in all creative acts. In Genesis 1:1-3 He is seen as ready to act as soon as the Word of God was given. (See Genesis 1:3,6,9,14,20,24.) The New Testament identifies this Word of God active in creation as Jesus (see John 1:1-4,14; Col. 1:16-17; Heb. 1:1-2).

God often uses physical realities as a tableau of corresponding spiritual realities. Here, Genesis 2:7 portrays Jesus bending over Adam and in the intimacy of love, kissing into him the gift of life, *neshamah,* through the Spirit, *ruach,* of God. The Holy Spirit entered into Adam and filled him with life. In so doing, the Holy Spirit animated the human spirit with His own life-giving energy. It follows, then, that the human spirit is not inherently immortal. It has no conscious existence apart from the life given it. Indeed, Paul for this very reason, and in order to combat this inference of Greek thought, refuses to talk about the human spirit at all until the person becomes a Christian.

## THE IMPACT OF SIN ON THE HUMAN SPIRIT

In His nocturnal conversation with Nicodemus, Jesus taught that the human spirit only comes alive to the things of God when it is born through the life-giving energy of the Holy Spirit from the world of God above. "Flesh gives birth to flesh, but the Spirit gives birth to spirit" (John 3:6). Notice the translators' distinction between the uppercase "S" ascribed to the Holy Spirit and the lowercase "s" ascribed to the human spirit. Paul draws the same distinction in his letter to the Ephesians. He describes the human spirit as under the control of satan and dead to the things of God, made alive solely by the initiative of God through His grace when the Gospel is heard and received (see Eph. 2:1-5). Not to have the Spirit of God is to be controlled by the spirit of "the ruler of the kingdom of the air, the spirit who is now at work in those who are disobedient" (Eph. 2:2).

For Paul, the human spirit is regarded as a gift of God's Spirit that is given to people when they accept the Gospel and believe in Jesus (see Rom. 8:15; 1 Cor. 2:11). He never at any stage mentions the word *spirit* in connection with a person who has not become a Christian. What he does do is consistently set the spirit over against what he calls the *flesh*. The Greek word for *flesh (sarx)* is a metaphor for human life lived apart from God, His presence, and His values. Paul does this intentionally. He only ever thinks in terms of the work of the Holy Spirit and perceives that the whole existence of the believer is determined by Him. The Spirit reveals to the believer the whole significance of what God has done through Jesus to deal with sin and put us right with Him again. He makes it possible for us to understand this and accept it. The Holy Spirit is always separate from the human spirit, but enables the human spirit to live for God rather than apart from Him. The Spirit of God becomes God's being for him because the believer no longer lives for his own being.

The apostle John emphasizes the same thing but in a different framework. He describes God and His world as inaccessible to people so long as they have not been enabled to do so by the Holy Spirit. This requires what John calls a "birth" of the human spirit in order to become a reality. This possibility has become available only through the coming of Jesus.

This being the case, it becomes clear that at the time sin entered earth's history the Holy Spirit ceased to naturally indwell the human spirit as He had previously done from the time of humankind's creation. Like a lover who had been rejected, the Spirit quietly withdrew from His habitation in Adam and Eve's human spirits. We have already discussed the impact of their fateful choice and the unfolding consequences on the realm of their bodies and their souls. The impact on their human spirits was far more disastrous.

The removal of the Holy Spirit left only the limited life-force of their human spirits in order to survive. With no indwelling contact with the eternal life-giving nature of God, that force gradually expended itself and finally ran out all together, eventuating in death, the ultimate nemesis of every human being to follow.

"...the wages of sin is death, but the gift of God is eternal life in Christ Jesus our Lord" (Rom. 6:23).

During its allotted time, the human spirit can still be stirred by various influences of the created world. Beautiful and powerful music almost invariably awakens passion of one type or another in the human spirit. Confronted with the overawing grandeur of nature with its kaleidoscope of subtle and vivid colors, and its magnitude of infinite variation, even a hardened spirit takes on a different sensibility, if only for one brief moment. The great speeches of notable orators down through the centuries stimulated the spirit of millions of people to follow their cause, noble or otherwise. The Bible often uses terminology such as "crushed" (Ps. 34:18), "anxious" (Job 7:11), "broken" (Job 17:1), "embittered" (Job 7:11), "faint" (Ps. 77:3), "failing" (Ps. 143:7), "haughty" (Prov. 16:18), "provoked" (Eccles. 7:9), "distressed" (Isa. 54:6), "despairing" (Isa. 61:3), "troubled" (Dan. 7:15), "timid," and "fearful" (2 Tim. 1:7) to describe the human spirit. Satan uses his power to harass and oppress the human spirit with strategies that he continually sets in place to discourage and destroy individuals.

By itself, however, there is one thing the human spirit can not do unaided, and that is respond naturally to the things of God or grasp what it is like in His realm above. This makes it impossible to worship God. The consistent metaphor used in Scripture to describe the human spirit in its relationship with God is "death" (see Eph. 2:1-5). Death by its very meaning implies the absence of life. It is only by the goodness of God's heart that He chooses to make the human spirit "alive." This only happens, however, when the human spirit chooses to respond to the life-giving words of the One who is the source of all life. These words proclaim His love for us and His mercy toward our rebellion. He has initiated a way in which the birth, life, death, resurrection, and high priestly ministry of Jesus is His means of granting forgiveness to human beings and putting them right with Him once again. As these things are heard, the creative life-giving Holy Spirit brings a sense of conviction to the nascent human spirit who now has the opportunity to respond to or reject the Spirit's wooing call (see John 16:7-15).

The apostle John describes it in these words: "…He came to His own people, but they didn't want Him. But whoever did want Him, who believed He was who He claimed and would do what He said, He made to be their true selves, their child-of-God selves. These are the God-begotten, not blood-begotten, not flesh-begotten, not sex-begotten" (John 1:11-13 TM). The same realities are expressed by John in other places in his Gospel.

> *God didn't go to all the trouble of sending His Son merely to point an accusing finger, telling the world how bad it was. He came to help, to put the world right again. Anyone who trusts in Him is acquitted; anyone who refuses to trust Him has long since been under the death sentence without knowing it. And why? Because of that person's failure to believe in the one-of-a-kind Son of God when introduced to Him. This is the crisis we're in: God-light streamed into the world, but men and women everywhere ran for the darkness. They went for the darkness because they were not really interested in pleasing God. Everyone who makes a practice of doing evil, addicted to denial and illusion, hates God-light and won't come near it, fearing a painful exposure. But anyone working and living in truth and reality welcomes God-light so the work can be seen for the God-work it is* (John 3:17-21 TM).

A physical analogy of this spiritual birthing is seen in the resurrection of Lazarus (see John 11:38-44). Lazarus had been dead for three days and his body was disintegrating in the heat of the Middle East. When Jesus cried, "Lazarus, come out," life once more surged into the dead man's body. The words of Jesus have an intangible quality of life whenever they are spoken. The same Holy Spirit who energized Jesus' commands at creation surged into Lazarus' inanimate being and gave it the gift of life once more. The same dynamic happens in the human spirit when, in a state of death to the things of God, the good news of what Jesus has done is proclaimed and penetrates the dead spirit bringing it to life. For the first time, it is able to respond to God and what He has to say.

## JESUS AND HIS HUMAN SPIRIT

We have discussed the circumstances of Jesus' birth and have been confronted with the reality that He was conceived by the Holy Spirit. That supernatural event of history in no way detracts from His genuine humanity. But it does emphasize that from His very human beginnings Jesus was indwelt by the Holy Spirit; much as, I believe, Adam received the breath of life at his creation. John the Baptist described Jesus as filled with the Holy Spirit "without limit" (John 3:34). There was never a time when Jesus' human spirit was not responsive to the things of His heavenly Father.

At His baptism, however, the Holy Spirit descended upon Jesus in a way that was different from merely indwelling Him as during the first thirty years of His life. It was a supernatural empowering for the ministry that lay ahead of Him and described in other passages of Scripture as an "anointing" (Acts 10:38, 4:26-27) for service. The genealogy of Jesus, which immediately follows the account of His baptism, is intentionally inserted at this place to emphasize His identification with Adam, the prototype human being (see Luke 3:38). Paul, on several occasions, identifies Jesus in this way, as the second Adam (Rom. 5:12-20; 1 Cor. 15:22), the new representative head of the human race. As such, Jesus was the forerunner of every human being whose human spirit can be empowered by the Holy Spirit's bestowal of spiritual gifts for serving God. The Gospel of Luke and the Book of Acts are both written by the same author as a two-part sequel. His Gospel describes the role of the Holy Spirit in Jesus' life and ministry, and the Book of Acts does the same thing regarding His followers. Every miracle performed by Jesus was also performed by human followers of Jesus.

Following His baptism, the Gospel of Luke consistently portrays Jesus as "full of the Holy Spirit" (Luke 4:1, 14-21). In His first sermon at the synagogue of His hometown, Nazareth, Jesus intentionally quotes a Messianic passage from Isaiah, claiming the Holy Spirit's anointing of Him at the Jordan to be the fulfillment of that prophecy before their very eyes (see Isa. 61:1-2). He was anointed to preach good news to the poor, to proclaim freedom for the prisoners, recovery of sight for the blind, and to release the oppressed. It becomes clear from these passages that Jesus did not perform a single one of His miracles from His divinity. He consistently did so as a Spirit-filled human being.

The apostle John says of Jesus in His humanity, "The Word became flesh and made his dwelling among us. We have seen his glory, the glory of the One and Only, who came from the Father, full of grace and truth" (John 1:14). The word *dwelling* is an allusion to the tabernacle built by Moses under God's instructions, which Jesus had previously alluded to as a symbol of His own human body (see John 2:19). The writer to the Hebrews also says the earthly sanctuary was "a copy and shadow of what is in heaven" [Jesus and His ministry] (Heb. 8:5). The outer covering of the sanctuary built in Moses' time was comprised of brown hides of sea cows (see Exod. 26:14) and hid the living Shekinah glory of the presence of God in the most Holy Place from the sight of the people camped outside. On the occasion of the temple's dedication, that glory was manifested outwardly and was so great that no human being could stand in its presence (see Exod. 40:34-35; 2 Chron. 7:1-3).

In the same way, the human body of Jesus was like a humble external covering for the glory of God hidden within, which manifested itself from time to time during His life. John says that the whole life of Jesus expressed the glory of God (see John 1:14), but in a spiritual sense it was His death that supremely manifested that glory (see John 12:23-33). The physical glory of the indwelling God also revealed itself on several occasions in Jesus' life. On the Mount of Transfiguration, Jesus' face shone like the sun (see Matt. 17:1-2). In the Garden of Gethsemane, the whole detachment of soldiers and some officials from the chief priests and Pharisees who had come to arrest Him, drew back and fell to the ground as He spoke (see John 18:1-6). Jesus, we have noticed, was constantly filled with the indwelling and empowering Holy Spirit without limit.

Jesus promised that He would ask the Father to send that same Holy Spirit to not only be externally "with" His followers by convicting them, wooing, and drawing them to Himself, but would eventually, some time in the future, be "in" them (see John 14:17).

Obviously, He would only come into them if He had at some time left them. This statement of Jesus confirms our earlier suppositions that the Holy Spirit had departed from indwelling humanity as sin entered the world. It certainly suggests that if the second Adam manifested outwardly the glory of the indwelling Holy Spirit from time to time, then such was probably also the case for the first Adam. The psalmist appears to endorse this. Quoting from the time God bestowed rulership on humankind at creation, he says:

> ...*You have set your glory above the heavens.* ...*When I consider Your heavens, the work of Your fingers, the moon and the stars, which You have set in place, what is man that You are mindful of him, the son of man that You care for him? You made him a little lower than the heavenly beings and crowned him with glory and honor. You made him ruler over the works of Your hands; you put everything under his feet...* (Psalm 8:1,3-6).

If this is indeed true, it is conceivable that the couple in Genesis 3:7 sewed fig leaves together primarily as a vain attempt to replace the covering of the glory emanating from the indwelling Holy Spirit, which I believe the Creator had breathed into them in His original bestowal of life as described in Genesis 2:7. It is significant that in Genesis 3:21 God gave them garments of skin to replace the fig leaves. In one sense, God would have been mercifully providing them with clothing more suitable than leaves against the elements of nature. But the main implication was almost certainly alluding to the introduction of the sacrificial system—an early tableau of the gospel. None of us can come into the presence of God in the stitching of our own human devising. We can only return to intimacy with Him through the covering He supplies for us through the death of the "Lamb of God," slain from the foundation of the world (John 1:29; Rev. 13:8).

## HUMAN "SPIRITUALITY"

God created human beings for intimacy with Him and to worship Him (see Gen. 2:1-3, 2:16-17, 3:8). When the human spirit does not worship God, it automatically seeks something or someone else to worship. On a basic level, anything that receives the ongoing focus of our attention above all else except God is a form of idolatry. God is replaced as first and foremost in our lives. The apostle Paul urges us to, "Put to death, therefore, whatever belongs to your earthly nature: sexual immorality, impurity, lust, evil desires and greed, which is idolatry" (Col. 3:5). Knowing how deeply ingrained in our spirits this proclivity is, God devoted the first four of the Ten Commandments to address the dangers of this reality.

Ultimately when all else fails, things and people and behaviors don't fill the inner need to worship in ways that satisfy the inner being (see Lev. 19:31; Deut. 18:9-15; 1 Sam. 28; Dan. 2:1-2; Mark 1:39). Paul graphically describes the consequence of intentional rejection of God's pleading through the Holy Spirit.

> But God's angry displeasure erupts as acts of human mistrust and wrongdoing and lying accumulate, as people try to put a shroud over truth. But the basic reality of God is plain enough. Open your eyes and there it is! By taking a long and thoughtful look at what God has created, people have always been able to see what their eyes as such can't see: eternal power, for instance, and the mystery of His divine being. So nobody has a good excuse. What happened was this: People knew God perfectly well, but when they didn't treat Him like God, refusing to worship Him, they trivialized themselves into silliness and confusion so that there was neither sense nor direction left in their lives. They pretended to know it all, but were illiterate regarding life. They traded the glory of God who holds the whole world in His hands for cheap figurines you can buy at any roadside stand (Romans 1:18-23 TM).

When, on the other hand, a human being does respond positively to the convicting and wooing power of the Holy Spirit as He brings home the compelling love of God as revealed in Jesus, then the human spirit is instantly and completely created anew (see 2 Cor. 5:17). This is what the Bible means when it uses the term *spiritual*. Gordon Fee compellingly clarifies what Paul's use of this term means and, at the same time, what it doesn't mean.[2]

He does **not mean:**

- religious (over against secular or mundane)

- non-material (spooky/ghostly)

- mystical (outside the world of reality)

- elitist (a spiritual Christian over against an everyday or carnal one)

- pertaining to the inner life of the believer (a focus on internal life)

However, he **does mean:**

...to be a Spirit person, one whose whole life is full of, and lived out by, the power of the Holy Spirit. Being "spiritual" then, is an adjective for the Holy Spirit; that which pertains to, or belongs to the Holy Spirit; rather than an adjective pertaining to a person.

For example, a spiritual gift is a gift of the Spirit (see Rom. 1:11); spiritual wisdom and insight are wisdom and insight from the Spirit (see Col. 1:9); spiritual songs are songs inspired by the Spirit (see Eph. 5:19) and spiritual blessings are blessings that come from life in the Spirit (see Eph. 1:3).

There is a different level of intimacy with God when Christians operate primarily from their Spirit-enlivened spirits. The Holy Spirit speaks to our human spirit and makes both prayer and guidance more personal (see Rom. 8:14-15; Isa. 30:21; Acts 8:29, 16:6-10). Nowhere is this interaction of the Holy Spirit with our human spirit illustrated better than in Paul's description in Romans chapter 8. He points out that before we become spiritual Christians we generally think of our relationship with God, if we actually have one, in terms of God as a slave master and we as His slaves. Even many believers in Christ function in their soul like someone who is not a Christian. They view their life as one needing to keep a set of moral rules that meets with stern punishment if not achieved.

The Holy Spirit changes that whole legalistic perspective and illuminates our spirit in a way that we are able to grasp the reality that we are actually sons or daughters of God rather than slaves.

That realization is not described as coming as some intellectual insight, but a crying out of the human spirit such as: "Wow, what freedom! You're actually my Abba, Father; not my slave master. I've never seen that before!" Peter expresses the same experience when he says, "Though you have not seen Him, you love Him; and even though you do not see Him now, you believe in Him and are filled with an inexpressible and glorious joy, for you are receiving the goal of your faith, the salvation of your souls" (1 Pet. 1:8-9).

## THE HUMAN SOUL AND THE HUMAN SPIRIT

Before opening our human spirit to the regenerating work of the Holy Spirit, we had functioned all of our lives from the locus of our souls outside of the Spirit of God and God's realm. We have described the strategies and dynamics human beings unconsciously choose, usually in early childhood, to cope with life without any input from the wisdom of God. As years pass, these self-centered strategies become deeply ingrained habits, entrenched physiologically in the butons of every synapse of the brain, and become increasingly destructive and counterproductive. And what is worse, they can never be removed until the second coming of Jesus and our human bodies are changed, and are no longer infected with the power of sin (see Rom. 8:22-25). Until that happens, they will continue to have the potential to wreak havoc in our lives.

The movement of the Holy Spirit from an external wooing to an internal blending with our own human spirits produces a life-giving impact and changes the previous dynamics all together. Along with embracing the Gospel, comes the power of God (see Rom. 1:16) to overcome sinfully based, destructive habits. From that moment on, however, there is an ongoing tension between these deeply ingrained habits in our humanity and the new Spirit-enlivened human spirit. The old habits don't give up easily and satan does his utmost to create circumstances that will constantly trigger them into reactivity if at all possible. This struggle is graphically described in the later parts of Paul's letter to the Galatians.

*My counsel is this: Live freely, animated and motivated by God's Spirit. Then you won't feed the compulsions of selfishness. For there is a root of sinful self-interest in us that is at odds with a free spirit, just as the free spirit is incompatible with selfishness. These two ways of life are antithetical, so that you cannot live at times one way and at times another way according to how you feel on any given day. Why don't you choose to be led by the Spirit and so escape the erratic compulsions of a law-dominated existence? It is obvious what kind of life develops out of trying to get your own way all the time: repetitive, loveless, cheap sex; a stinking accumulation of mental and emotional garbage; frenzied and joyless grabs for happiness; trinket gods; magic-show religion; paranoid loneliness; cutthroat competition; all-consuming-yet-never-satisfied wants; a brutal temper; an impotence to love or be loved; divided homes and divided lives; small-minded and lopsided pursuits; the vicious habit of depersonalizing everyone into a rival; uncontrolled and uncontrollable addictions; ugly parodies of community. I could go on. This isn't the first time I have warned you, you know. If you use your freedom this way, you will not inherit God's kingdom. But what happens when we live God's way? He brings gifts into our lives, much the same way that fruit appears in an orchard—things like affection for others, exuberance about life, serenity. We develop a willingness to stick with things, a sense of compassion in the heart, and a conviction that a basic holiness permeates things and people. We find ourselves involved in loyal commitments, not needing to force our way in life, able to marshal and direct our energies wisely. Legalism is helpless in bringing this about; it only gets in the way. Among those who belong to Christ, everything connected with getting our own way and mindlessly responding to what everyone else calls necessities is killed off for good—crucified. Since this is the kind of life we have chosen, the life of the Spirit, let us make sure that we do not just hold it as an idea in our heads or a sentiment in our hearts, but work out its implications in every detail of our lives. That means we will not compare ourselves with each other as if one of us were better and another worse. We have far more interesting things to do with our lives. Each of us is an original* (Galatians 5:16-26 TM).

This passage underlines the ongoing struggle between the newly created spiritual Christian and the old embedded structures which linger on from the unconverted era of that person's life. Paul tells us clearly how to deal with the old nature. Its passions and desires are to be crucified, rather than modified by human effort. By this, he means that through faith we identify our old sinful nature with the crucified life of Christ (see Rom. 6:1-14) and render it inoperative. At the same time, we are to identify our present lives through faith with the resurrected Spirit-filled life of Jesus. To live in the Spirit, he says, means to keep in step with the Spirit. From a practical perspective, that requires us to nurture and feed the relationship of our human spirits with the Holy Spirit in an ongoing way. Authors such as Richard Foster and Dallas Willard give us many helpful guidelines on such spiritual discipline.[3]

## THE HOLY SPIRIT'S INDWELLING AND EMPOWERING

The fruitage that becomes evident in the human spirit from nurturing an indwelling relationship with the Holy Spirit is such that the Christian becomes more habitually like Jesus. Love, joy, peace, patience, kindness, goodness, faithfulness, gentleness, and self-control are all qualities that Jesus manifested in His Spirit-filled life.

The Holy Spirit ministers to our inner life in several ways. As we cultivate a continuing intimacy with each member of the Trinity, not only does the Spirit's indwelling activity in our human spirits bear fruitage, but when needs for Christian ministry and service arise, the Holy Spirit will also empower us with spiritual gifts necessary for the task of extending the Kingdom of God (see 1 Cor. 12:1-31; Rom. 12:3-8; Eph. 4:1-16).

There is a profound difference between the fruit of the Holy Spirit and the gifts of the Holy Spirit.

— The Spirit's indwelling is designed to mature us, causing us to grow in the Lord; whereas the Spirit's empowering is designed to equip us, enabling us to serve the Lord.

— The Spirit indwells to give us victory over sin, making us holy; whereas the Spirit empowers us to give us tools for ministry, making us effective.

— The Spirit lives within us to give us the character of Christ; whereas the Spirit comes upon us in power to give us the ministry of Christ.

The distinctive characteristics of the Spirit's *indwelling* are:

♦ It is received automatically at conversion (see Gal. 3:2).

♦ It does not have to be prayed for, or sought by begging, pleading, or fasting (see 1 Pet. 1:3-5).

♦ It is not overtly experiential; it is not necessarily accompanied by feelings or sensations (see John 3:8,16).

♦ It is accepted by faith (see Rom. 3:22).

♦ It has no supernatural manifestations or release of charismatic gifts (see 1 Cor. 7:40).

♦ There is a quiet work focusing on assurance, obedience, repentance, and spiritual growth (see Acts 2:36-39).

♦ It is an ongoing gradual process of growth in holiness (see Gal. 5:22-23).

♦ The fruit is primarily an illumination of the Word of God and growth in Christian living (see John 16:13).

The distinctive characteristics of the Spirit's *empowering*, however, are:

♦ It is experiential, spasmodic, and repeated (see Acts 4:19-31).

♦ It can be seen and heard (Acts 2:32-33).

- It is referred to as "coming upon, falling on, and poured out on" (see Acts 10:44 KJV; 11:15 KJV; 2:33).

- Spiritual gifts are bestowed as needed (see 1 Cor. 12:4-11).

- Power is given to overcome obstacles (see Acts 5:1-5).

- It is usually given for an evangelistic purpose (see 1 Cor. 2:1-5).

- It usually comes by asking and impartation (see Luke 11:11-13; 2 Tim. 1:6-7).

- It is used for the good of the Church as a whole rather than personal ego (see 1 Cor. 14:26; Eph. 4:14-16).

The Bible is clear, however, that the gifts of the Spirit can be abused, and because of this the *fruit* of the Spirit has a priority over the *gifts* of the Spirit from God's perspective. The contrast in these two workings of the Holy Spirit was dramatically displayed in the church at Corinth. Paul spends three chapters of his first letter to them spelling out the supremacy of love over the members' use of the gift of tongues as a measure of superior spirituality. Unless love was evident in their relationships, any gifting was just a resounding gong or a clanging cymbal (see 1 Cor. 13:1-3).

That does not mean that spiritual gifts are irrelevant for the Christian. In the same passage, Paul urges the Corinthians to, "Follow the way of love and eagerly desire spiritual gifts, especially the gift of prophecy" (1 Cor. 14:1). When the fruits of the Spirit were evident in a congregation, then the gifts of the Spirit could be used for mutual edification. Prophecy is singled out because this was especially given to strengthen, encourage, and comfort the church (see 1 Cor. 14:3).

From all that has been discussed, we can see the crucial importance of living from the perspective of the human spirit that has come alive through the Holy Spirit's work. To miss this vital issue is to miss two things: what God offers us through the ministry of Jesus to make us one with Him again, and the inheritance the Holy Spirit wants to share with us.

# ENDNOTES

1. Gerhard Kittel and Gerhard Friedrich, eds., *Theological Dictionary of the New Testament* (Grand Rapids, MI: Eerdmans Publishing Company, 1974), 332-451.

2. Gordon Fee, *God's Empowering Presence* (Peabody, MA: Hendrickson Publishers, 2002), 14-32.

3. Richard Foster, *Celebration of Discipline* (London, UK, Hodder & Stoughton, 1984).
   Dallas Willard, *The Spirit of the Disciplines* (London, UK, Hodder & Stoughton, 1988).

# CHAPTER TEN

# THE FULLNESS OF
# OUR INHERITANCE

# THE FULLNESS OF
# OUR INHERITANCE

*...But I do more than thank. I ask—ask the God of our Master,
Jesus Christ, the God of glory—to make you intelligent and dis-
cerning in knowing Him personally, your eyes focused and clear, so
that you can see exactly what it is He is calling you to do, grasp the
immensity of this glorious way of life He has for Christians, oh, the
utter extravagance of His work in us who trust Him—endless energy, boundless strength! All this energy issues from Christ: God
raised Him from death and set Him on a throne in deep heaven, in
charge of running the universe, everything from galaxies to governments, no name and no power exempt from His rule. And not just
for the time being, but forever. He is in charge of it all, has the final
word on everything. At the center of all this, Christ rules the
church. The church, you see, is not peripheral to the world; the
world is peripheral to the church. The church is Christ's body, in
which He speaks and acts, by which He fills everything with His
presence* (Ephesians 1:17-23 TM).

Paul's letter to the Ephesians is majestically cosmic in its perspective. It lifts our vision to the eternal realities ushered in by the
life, death, and resurrection of Jesus and then seeks to apply them to
the everyday issues of life that we encounter as Christians. Chapter
1 is full of superlatives in praise for Jesus and what He has accom-
plished for the human race. The key expression is "in Christ," a
phrase or its equivalent which is found in nearly every verse of the

first half of the chapter. It is imperative to grasp and internalize the meaning of this biblical term in order to apply its significance to everyday living.

The term *in Christ* is similar in meaning to the legal agreement that two people commit to when they enter into a covenant relationship with each other at marriage. Although covenants form the national and spiritual fabric of the Old Testament, marriage is still the classic experience that models this best for those of us living in the twenty-first century. In the marriage covenant, the husband and wife share all of their assets. What belongs to one, also legally belongs to the other, unless designated otherwise. To be in Christ means that Jesus shares all that He is, and has, and has done, with us. Verse 13 (NIV) indicates that we become in Christ when we hear "the word of truth, the gospel of your salvation" and internalize it through meaningful belief. This is the spiritual equivalent of a bride accepting her heavenly Bridegroom and all that went along with His commitment to her.

The first stunning asset Paul says we share with Jesus at that moment of belief is a "deposit" or "down payment" of the Holy Spirit which enables us to experience the reality of the Kingdom of God in a partial sense. Ultimately, we will receive our full inheritance when He returns again and fully claims those He has purchased from satan at the cost of His own life on the cross (see Eph. 1:14). As such, the Holy Spirit is called a seal of the Bridegroom's integrity and a guarantee that we will one day share fully in all that is totally His. As Christians, we can claim by faith now, and experience as a reality in the present moment, elements of our final inheritance through the ministry of the indwelling Holy Spirit. It is as experiential as "tasting" food (see Heb. 6:4-6).

The tragedy is that most of us never inherit the down payment let alone the full payment of our inheritance. We don't possess our legal possessions. We allow the pressures of life to crowd out our awareness of what is rightfully ours and offered freely to us. Paul is so concerned about this that in verse 17 he begins a passionate and extended prayer for the Holy Spirit to give us wisdom and revelation, so that we may know Him better. This knowledge is not intellectual knowledge. It is the experiential knowledge that the Bible describes when Adam "knew" his wife Eve and she conceived. Paul wants us to know our bridegroom in just that way.

He continues to pray that "...you can see exactly what it is He is calling you to do, grasp the immensity of this glorious way of life He has for Christians, oh, the utter extravagance of His work in us who trust Him—endless energy, boundless strength! All this energy issues from Christ." In order to understand the magnitude of that inheritance, one that is available to us right now, Paul spells it out in graphic detail. "All this energy issues from Christ: God raised Him from death and set Him on a throne in deep heaven, in charge of running the universe, everything from galaxies to governments, no name and no power exempt from His rule. And not just for the time being, but forever. He is in charge of it all, has the final word on everything..." (Eph. 1:20 TM).

The implications of this are staggering. Our inheritance includes the power that raised Jesus from the grave and seated Him in Heaven beside the Father. Ephesians 2:6 indicates that in Christ we are actually seated with Him in the heavenly realms right at this moment. More than that, we are seated with Christ in His finished victory over satan and all the evil powers and dominions he had set up in his endeavors to overcome Jesus. By faith we can taste experientially the essence of the age to come that has been ushered in by Jesus. God placed all things under Jesus' feet and appointed Him head over everything. We miss the whole thrust of this chapter if we overlook the next few words, "At the center of all this, Christ rules the church. The church, you see, is not peripheral to the world; the world is peripheral to the church. The church is Christ's body, in which He speaks and acts, by which He fills everything with His presence" (Eph. 1:20 TM). All of these accomplishments of Jesus are specifically dedicated to the church for its everyday life and ministry in the world. Using the metaphor of the human body once again, Jesus is described as the head with His feet trampling on a defeated opponent. We are called upon to be His body and flesh out the fullness of who Christ is and what He has done in every way.

*Oh Father, forgive us for being so short sighted and as a consequence, so impotent in the realms of everyday life…in marriage, parenthood, and business, and for not facing the issues of spiritual warfare with boldness and confidence, for not implementing all You have made available for us and want us to employ.*

We did not really need Paul to explain this to us. Jesus Himself had already articulated it in detail when He delivered the Gospel commission to the disciples and every follower of His down through subsequent history. He came to them in Galilee after His resurrection just prior to His ascension to Heaven, and said, "…All authority in heaven and on earth has been given to Me. Therefore go and make disciples of all nations, baptizing them in the name of the Father and of the Son and of the Holy Spirit, and teaching them to obey everything I have commanded you. And surely I am with you always, to the very end of the age" (Matt. 28:18-20).

The spiritual realities open to all aspects of human nature as depicted in the New Testament are somehow not grasped by many of those attending church these days. Some are locked into a Christian rationalism heavily rooted in the soul. They live in a world of intellectual statements of belief which, like the Jews of Jesus' day, define what is approved and what isn't.

Others are buffeted by a tumult of variable emotions, seeking but never finding an ongoing experience of hyped-up emotional excitement, a continual high, that they hope will eventually give them assurance of their relationship with God. Still, others find themselves chained by the bondage of performance, choosing behaviors that can only bind them into a critical comparison with their peers in order to gauge the level of their own achievement. Soulish Christianity never delivers the inheritance offered to the Christian who functions first and foremost from a human spirit that has been indwelt and empowered by the Holy Spirit with all the freedom and joy that ensues (see Jer. 2:13).

We need to open the eyes of our heart to see afresh the dominating thrust of the New Testament. It consistently and confrontively describes the Christian era as the age of the Holy Spirit.

First Corinthians chapter 2 spells this out as clearly as God has ever done in His Word. Paul here contrasts two forms of wisdom: a soulish "wisdom" characteristic of the rulers of this present age who ultimately crucified Jesus, and a mature wisdom that is revealed to Christians by the Holy Spirit. "We have not received the spirit of the world" Paul says, "but the Spirit who is from God, lets us in on it. God offers a full report on the gifts of life and salvation that he is giving us. We don't have to rely on the world's guesses and opinions. We didn't learn this by reading books or going to school; we learned it from God, who taught us person-to-person through Jesus, and we're passing it on to you in the same firsthand, personal way. The unspiritual self, just as it is by nature, can't receive the gifts of God's Spirit. There's no capacity for them. They seem like so much silliness. Spirit can be known only by spirit—God's Spirit and our spirits in open communion (see 1 Cor. 2:12-14 TM).

The two wisdoms cannot co-exist. When confronted by the divine wisdom of Christ with an insistence they could no longer deny or sweep under the carpet, the leaders of His time chose to deal with their dilemma by seeking to destroy Him and His wisdom. We have pointed out that the Holy Spirit gives us the mind of Jesus, to think like Jesus, to see life from Jesus' perspective and His values, and ultimately to love like Jesus. Whenever Christians manifest the mind of Christ and His wisdom, they too will encounter the same spirit of opposition. Scripture emphasizes that "…our struggle is not against flesh and blood, but against the [same] rulers, against the authorities, against the powers of this dark world and against the spiritual forces of evil in the heavenly realms" that Jesus encountered (Eph. 6:12).

The activity of the Holy Spirit on the human spirit experiences much opposition from these sources. The power of the Spirit to regenerate the human spirit can be resisted (see Acts 7:57). The power of the Holy Spirit to fill the human spirit for intimacy can be grieved (see Eph. 4:30). And the power of the Holy Spirit to empower the human spirit for ministry and service can be quenched (see 1 Thess. 5:19). This happens continually in the lives of individual Christians and Christian institutions alike.

Generally speaking, white, Western cultures have a fear of the supernatural or the unknown. The human soul invariably wants to remain in control of life. If we welcome the presence of the Spirit into our lives, there is no way we can remain in control of the way things work out. Sometimes deeply ingrained habits and long-standing traditions stubbornly resist changes that come with the presence of the Spirit. Many Christian institutions and individuals choose programs, plans, initiatives, and human energies to try and accomplish God's work, rather than first taking time to seek and discern His agenda at the time. Institutional and church committees always face the danger of shackling initiatives the Spirit may birth through the inevitable dynamic of red tape. His mode of operating is usually spontaneous and cuts across all natural barriers of the human soul. He often confronts and challenges our public image, which is very conscious of appearances and invariably focused inward. God often confounds the mind to reveal the real nature of the human spirit.

Nowhere is this illustrated more than in Second Corinthians chapter 3. In this chapter, Paul is contrasting the two forms of religious experiences, one from the Jewish nation who rejected Christ as the Messiah and continued to live their lives "under the letter of Old Testament law," and the other from the disciples who had accepted Jesus as the Messiah and lived their lives under the indwelling and empowering presence of the Holy Spirit.

> ...[God's] letter authorizes us to help carry out this new plan of action. The plan wasn't written out with ink on paper, with pages and pages of legal footnotes, killing your spirit. It's written with Spirit on spirit, His life on our lives! The Government of Death, its constitution chiseled on stone tablets, had a dazzling inaugural. Moses' face as he delivered the tablets was so bright that day (even though it would fade soon enough) that the people of Israel could no more look right at him than stare into the sun. How much more dazzling, then, the Government of Living Spirit? If the Government of Condemnation was impressive, how about this Government of Affirmation? Bright as that old government was, it would look downright dull alongside this new one. If that makeshift arrangement impressed us, how much more this brightly shining

*government installed for eternity? With that kind of hope to excite us, nothing holds us back. Unlike Moses, we have nothing to hide. Everything is out in the open with us. He wore a veil so the children of Israel wouldn't notice that the glory was fading away— and they didn't notice. They didn't notice it then and they don't notice it now, don't notice that there's nothing left behind that veil. Even today when the proclamations of that old, bankrupt government are read out, they can't see through it. Only Christ can get rid of the veil so they can see for themselves that there's nothing there. Whenever, though, they turn to face God as Moses did, God removes the veil and there they are—face to face! They suddenly recognize that God is a living, personal presence, not a piece of chiseled stone. And when God is personally present, a living Spirit, that old, constricting legislation is recognized as obsolete. We're free of it! All of us! Nothing between us and God, our faces shining with the brightness of His face. And so we are transfigured much like the Messiah, our lives gradually becoming brighter and more beautiful as God enters our lives and we become like Him* (2 Corinthians 3:6-18 TM).

It is extremely profitable to analyze in detail the characteristics of the two forms of ministry that Paul is talking about. The first, which he earlier describes as having the "smell of death" hanging over it, administered the requirements for living that God spelled out for us in the Ten Commandments (see 2 Cor. 3:15-16). They tried to live by the letter of impersonal laws written on tablets of stone. That encounter with God was so glorious that Moses' face shone with glory for some time when he came down from the mountain with the tablets. But it ultimately condemned people and brought them under a sentence of death because they could not fulfill what it required of them. Because of the power of sin which dwells in our human nature, nobody can ever keep the inner principles of the Ten Commandments the way God wants us to. The glory always fades.

In the days when Jesus was on earth, dullness hung over the minds of people who rejected Him as the Messiah and prevented their human spirits from coming alive to the things of God as He wanted.

As such, they were kept in continual bondage trying to reach a standard of morality beyond their reach.

The second form of ministry, which Paul described as a "fragrance of life," brings the presence of God Himself into the human spirit. The author of God's requirements dwells intimately within. No longer do His requirements stand impersonally outside them, condemning them. Through the Spirit's ministry, the requirements of God are written on human hearts rather than inanimate stone, bringing a dimension of heartfelt closeness to God that transcends any legal obligation. Instead of death, it brings life to the human spirit. Its glory surpasses that manifested on Mount Sinai because it brings with it an attitude to living which springs spontaneously from the inner heart and lasts forever. The veil of spiritual dullness is removed, and the Scriptures come alive when they are read. The human spirit has a sense of freedom instead of bondage because it trusts the presence of the living Lord. Such a freedom never leads a Christian to presumptuously disregard God's will as He has revealed it in the Ten Commandments.

The major underlying difference between the two ways of living is seen in what, or who, they received as lord. The former group looked to rules as lord of their human souls, while the latter group looked to the Holy Spirit as Lord of their human souls.

In saying all this, Paul does not imply that the Holy Spirit replaces the work of Christ. He can never do that. It was Jesus who came to this planet and lived and died and rose again for our salvation. All the Holy Spirit does is internalize everything that Jesus has done for us and flesh it out in our everyday life. He does this in a very personal way by mingling inwardly with our human spirit.

The Holy Spirit is the Spirit of Jesus. He makes Jesus real to us and enables us to experience—really experience—intimacy with Him. Christianity, in the final analysis, is Christ-centered and Spirit-filled, revealing the heart of the Father. In a moving moment on the last day of the Feast of Tabernacles, Jesus stood and cried out in a loud voice, "'...If anyone thirsts, let him come to Me and drink. Rivers of living water will brim and spill out of the depths of anyone who believes in Me this way, just as the Scripture says.' (He said this in regard to the Spirit, whom those who believed in Him were about to receive. The Spirit had not yet been given because Jesus had not yet been glorified" (John 7:37-39 TM).

As the human spirit surrenders to the wooing of the Holy Spirit, who then takes up residence within, the human soul surrenders itself to a new Lord. Dysfunctional thinking patterns, crippled emotional responses, and destructive addictive behavioral choices are all submitted to the Holy Spirit who now reigns in the individual's life instead of self-centered desires and motives. The body, also, is yielded to the indwelling Spirit and becomes a living temple where the living Lord now dwells, as He once did in the temple erected in Jerusalem. In that Hebrew temple, animals were put to death as a symbol of the death that Jesus would ultimately die; but now, the way Christians live is called a living sacrifice (see Rom. 12:2). The different parts and organs of the human body are now used as instruments to perform God's will, and in a way symbolized by streams of living water. The Holy Spirit flows out of the Christian as an agent to heal others.

The following illustration explains:

body                          soul                          spirit

At conversion, the Holy Spirit's work of bringing the human spirit to life is instantaneous, total, and complete. "If anyone is in

Christ, he is a new creation; the old has gone, the new has come!" (2 Cor. 5:17). So begins a slow but progressive transformation of every element of the soul. It is a time of transition, a time of ongoing healing. "...be transformed" Paul says, "by the renewing of your mind" (Rom. 12:2). The body alone, in its existing form, does not change for the better. It awaits the fulfillment of God's saving work at the second coming of Jesus. "...flesh and blood cannot inherit the kingdom of God..." (1 Cor. 15:50).

As we bring this reflection to a close, it is evident that there is an urgent and great need for us to rediscover the reality of the spiritual realm, the reality of spiritual experience, and the reality of spiritual warfare. Not to do so locks us into a truncated and nonbiblical form of Christianity that can never fulfill what it has potential to do and binds us into a form of religious humanism.

# EPILOGUE

# EPILOGUE

This book has focused on aspects of human nature as we experience them in our present life. The Bible, however, presents another dimension of these aspects of humanity in the life to come and it would be remiss if this work concluded without reflecting on the hope held out to all Christians.

## THE HUMAN BODY

Christians living in the city of Corinth were heavily influenced by Greek thinking of their time and had trouble coming to terms with Christianity's emphasis on the resurrection of the human body at the end of earth's history when Jesus returns. Many had abandoned the hope of a literal bodily resurrection in the face of Paul's clear teaching on this issue when he had first founded the church. They tried to harmonize this belief with the common ideas accepted by their surrounding pagan Greek culture. They claimed that they were already experiencing a resurrected life as a Christian, and that this was all anybody could ever expect (see 1 Cor. 15:1-34).

The apostle Paul spends a major section of First Corinthians chapter 15 addressing the error of their beliefs. He began by confirming the report of many reliable witnesses of Christ's bodily resurrection and the undeniable history of this event as foundational to Christianity. Christ's resurrection is held up as the firstfruits and the prototype of the general resurrection of the dead to follow at the end of time (see 1 Cor. 15:20).

Paul then spends a major section of the chapter describing the actual nature of the resurrected human body at that time (see 1 Cor. 15:35-58).[1] He begins by describing the infinite variety of physical bodies God has created in nature, with a specific emphasis on how some of these bodies are transformed through the different stages of their growth cycle. He uses this illustration as a springboard to describe the nature of the human body after its resurrection. He is at pains to point out that it will still be in bodily form but certainly not identical to its present form in this age.

The characteristics Paul ascribes to the human body as it exists now are "sown," "perishable," "dishonour," "weakness," and "natural." In contrast to these traits, the resurrected body is described as "raised" (continuing to exist in a bodily form but different in nature), "imperishable" (not subject to death or decay), "glorious" (not marked by the indignities associated with our present existence), "powerful" (in contrast to the weakness of the present body), and "spiritual" (a supernatural body filled with the Holy Spirit rather than one tainted with sin).

This echoes a corresponding statement Paul made when he said, "...our citizenship is in heaven. And we eagerly await a Savior from there, the Lord Jesus Christ, who, by the power that enables Him to bring everything under His control, will transform our lowly bodies so that they will be like His glorious body" (Phil. 3:20-21). We have already noticed that Jesus' body after the resurrection continued to be corporeal, but in some ways different to the body He had before His death. He could, for example, walk through locked doors, appear and disappear, and ascend to Heaven.

These are the dynamics that Paul describes in First Corinthians 15 as "spiritual." "Supernatural" is probably a better translation on this occasion rather than "spiritual." The contrast is not between something material or ghostly, but between earth and Heaven; between the sorts of life characterized by Adam in his existence on earth and Jesus' existence in Heaven after His resurrection.

One thing is made very clear, however—"flesh and blood" as it exists now cannot inherit the Kingdom of God. It must be miraculously transformed at the second coming of Jesus. In a moment of time heralded by the trumpet of God, the dead who died with faith in Christ will be resurrected to life as has been described, and those still living at that time will be instantly transformed and translated together with the resurrected dead, to be with Christ forever (see 1 Thess. 4:13-18). The sting of death that has up until this moment relentlessly and systematically destroyed every human body infected with sin, has been defeated forever through the firstfruits of Jesus' death and His resurrection "for" us. He has been our representative substitute in every sense.

The Old Testament anticipated a somewhat similar end-time change in human nature but within a different framework. (See Isaiah 65:17-25.) In contrast to the radical and instantaneous creation of a new Heaven and a new earth at the end of time portrayed in the New Testament, the Old Testament looked forward to a gradual progressive transformation of life on earth resulting from the nation of Israel's acceptance of their Messiah. With their failure to receive Jesus as the Messiah, God inaugurated a new covenant with a new "Israel." Racial distinctions no longer defined who was a member of God's people. A person became a member of Israel, in a spiritual sense, when he or she demonstrated the same faith in God that Abraham, the national biological father of Israel, had demonstrated. They inherited all the spiritual promises and responsibilities originally given to national Israel (see Gal. 3:28-29; Rom. 2:26-29, 4:1-25).

A study of Jesus' life and ministry makes it clear that He was intentionally establishing a symbolic new Israel to replace the old national Israel who were about to reject Him and crucify Him. Jesus became the one "true" Israel who fulfilled all that God desired national Israel to carry out. As a child, for example, Jesus went into Egypt like Israel had done beforehand and returned to the Promised Land (see Matt. 2:13-23). Like Moses, He went up onto a mountain and shared a deeper understanding of the Ten Commandments (Matt. 5-7) in the Sermon on the Mount. There came a time during

His ministry when He intentionally selected twelve apostles to replace the twelve tribes of Israel in a symbolic manner. The central truth of Christianity is that if we have become in Christ through belief in Him, then we too comprise the one true Israel and receive the privileges and responsibilities of Israel (see Eph. 1:3-14).

All the promises and responsibilities that God had initially ascribed to national Israel in the Old Testament are transferred onto the Christian church in the New Testament (see 1 Pet. 2:4-10; Heb. 8:1-13). God laid aside what became known as the "old" covenant with His chosen people and established a "new" covenant with those He regarded effectively as a new Israel, a spiritual Israel. His outpouring of the Holy Spirit at Pentecost validated this new Israel (see Acts 2:32-33, 11:1-18).

One more thing needs to be said about resurrection of the dead. Jesus clearly taught that all human beings would be resurrected at some time in the future, whether they had faith in Him or not. "Do not be amazed at this, for a time is coming when all who are in their graves will hear His voice and come out—those who have done good will rise to live, and those who have done evil will rise to be condemned" (John 5:28-29). The Book of Revelation makes it clear that these two resurrections are actually separated by a period of 1,000 years (see Rev. 20:5). During the thousand years, those who have been resurrected when Jesus comes are described as involved in some form of judgment. Paul spells out that that occasion involves the judgment of evil angels and the vindication of God's character in the face of the cosmic slander satan has continually directed at Him down through the ages (see Rev. 20:4-6; 1 Cor. 6:1-11).

The resurrection at the end of the 1,000 years, comprising all those who have never embraced Jesus as the Messiah, does not seem to involve any change in their human bodies. They emerge from their graves exactly as they went down into them, with hearts committed to independence from God and rebellion against Him. Satan persuades them to join him in a concerted endeavor to overthrow God. Their plans are thwarted by the final judgment, which is similar in its vindication of all that God has done to offer them salvation. Their ultimate destiny is a second death from which there is no resurrection (see Rev. 20:5-15).

## THE HUMAN SOUL

Even in its present condition, the human soul has amazing capabilities to learn and develop new insights into the world around us. Knowledge and technology has entered an exponential line of growth in every area of learning and the sciences. It almost seems a contradiction that mental and emotional dysfunction is also increasing exponentially while other circumstances on the planet are relentlessly disintegrating in human areas of sociology, world economy, ecological disasters, and seemingly unsolvable political and military conflicts. The pressures and stresses on the human mind to solve these dilemmas are producing an enormous rise in emotional disorders and destructive choices in the vain hope of blotting out the resulting pain of life in general.

We have seen already that this is due to the crippling effect of a moral cancer that came with the impact of sin on the human race. Thinking patterns were clouded, emotional reactions were darkened, and behavioral choices were corrupted.

With the inner change that comes with Christian conversion, all these crippled aspects of the soul have access to a power which can begin a process of healing to its woundedness. As we saturate ourselves in the Word of God and the guidance of the Holy Spirit, we are increasingly given the mind of Christ (see 1 Cor. 2:16). We grow to think like Him and view life from His perspective, with His heart for all things. Through the faithful and ongoing practice of spiritual disciplines, the soul is gradually transformed in a process that is ongoing.

At the second coming of Christ and the resurrection of the body which, from this time, is no longer tainted with the inner corruption of sin, the soul faces the promise of unlimited growth for the rest of eternity. There will always be new things to learn as each person continues to reach into the unsearchable riches of Christ that can never be exhausted.

## The Human Spirit

As mentioned previously, at the time of conversion, God gives humans the quality of life manifested in the age to come. He does not say that upon belief in Jesus as the unique Son of God, He will give us eternal life some time in the future. We "have" eternal life from the moment we commit our lives to Him (see John 3:16). Out of His deep love for us, He "has made us alive" with Christ (Eph. 2:4-5). "…if anyone is in Christ, he is a new creation; the old has gone, the new has come" (2 Cor. 5:17).

In the tensions and pressures of everyday life, Christians may not always sense the reality of that new life they have received, but it is there, nevertheless. From time to time in their walk with Christ, they may taste it in all its fullness (see Heb. 6:4-6). But this is only spasmodic in character; to encourage us, Paul prayed earnestly that the Holy Spirit would open the eyes of our inner being to constantly perceive the realities of the Holy Spirit's presence in our lives (see Eph. 1:17-18). We can have that assurance because Jesus is a life-giving spirit (see 1 Cor. 15:5), and we will share that same life-giving Spirit throughout eternity. There will be no flaming sword keeping us from the tree of life in the earth made new (see Gen. 3:24; Rev. 22:1-2).

## Endnote

1. Paul Beasley-Murray, *The Message of the Resurrection* (Leicester, UK: InterVarsity Press, 2000), 137-146.

# Appendix A

# THE TRUE IDENTITY OF OUR SOUL "IN CHRIST"

## I Am Accepted in Christ

- I am God's child (John 1:12).

- I am Christ's best friend (John 15:15).

- I have been justified (Rom. 5:1).

- I am united with the Lord, and I am one spirit with Him (1 Cor. 6:17).

- I have been bought with a price; I belong to Him (1 Cor. 6:19-20).

- I am a member of Christ's body (1 Cor. 12: 27).

- I am a saint, a holy one (Eph. 1:1).

- I have been adopted as God's child (Eph. 1:5).

- I have direct access to God through the Holy Spirit (Eph. 2:18).

- I have been redeemed and forgiven of all my sins (Col. 1:14).

- I am complete in Christ (Col. 2:10).

## I AM SECURE IN CHRIST

- I am free forever from condemnation (Rom. 8:1-12).

- I am assured that all things work together for my good (Rom. 8:28).

- I am free from any condemning charges against me (Rom. 8:31-34).

- I cannot be separated from the love of Christ (Rom. 8:35-39).

- I have been established (made firm), anointed, and sealed by God (2 Cor. 1:21-22).

- I am confident the good work God has begun in me will be perfected (Phil. 1:6).

- I am a citizen of heaven (Phil. 3:20).

- I am hidden with Christ in God (Col. 3:3).

- I have not been given a spirit of fear but of power, love, and a sound mind (2 Tim. 1:7).

- I can find grace and mercy to help in time of need (Heb. 4:16).

- I am born of God, and the evil one cannot touch me (1 John 5:18).

## I AM SIGNIFICANT IN CHRIST

- I am the salt of the earth and the light of the world (Matt. 5:13-14).

- I am a branch of the true vine, Jesus, and a channel of His life (John 15:1-5).

- I have been chosen and appointed by God to bear fruit (John 15:16).

- I am a personal, Spirit-empowered witness of Christ (Acts 1:8).

- I am a temple of God (1 Cor. 3:16).

- I am a minister of reconciliation for God (2 Cor. 5:17-21).

- I am God's co-worker (2 Cor. 6:1).

- I am seated with Christ in the heavenly realm (Eph. 2:6).

- I am God's workmanship, created for good works (Eph. 2:10).

- I may approach God with freedom and confidence (Eph. 3:12).

- I can do all things through Christ who strengthens me (Phil. 4:13).

- By the grace of God, I am what I am (1 Cor. 15:10).

*Source Unknown*

# RECOMMENDED READING

- Beasley-Murray, Paul. *The Message of the Resurrection.* Leicester, UK: Inter-Varsity Press, 2000.

- Beesing, Maria; Nogosek, Robert J.; O'Leary, Patrick H. *The Enneagram.* Denville, NJ: Dimension Books, 2006.

- Cullmann, Oscar. *Immortality of the Soul or Resurrection of the Dead?* http://www.religion-online.org/showbook.asp?title=1115; accessed October 6, 2009.

- Eusebius (VII, xxv) see http://www.newadvent.org/fathers/250107.htm; and Tertullian (De carne Christi, xxiv) see Septimii Florentis Tertulliani De Carne Christi Liber, *Tertullian's Treatise on the Incarnation,* text edited with Introduction, Translation, and Commentary by Ernest Evans, D.D., Oxford, Hon. D.D. Glasgow, Vicar of Hellifield and Canon of Radford, London, S.P.C.K, 1956.

- Fee, Gordon. *God's Empowering Presence.* Peabody MA: Hendrickson Publishers, 2002.

- Foster, Richard. *Celebration of Discipline.* London: Hodder & Stoughton, 1984.

- Hendrix, H. *Keeping the Love You Find.* New York: Pocket Books, 1992.

- Henslin, E.R. *Forgiven and Free.* Nashville, TN: Thomas Nelson, 1978.

- Kittel, Gerhard; Friedrich, Gerhard, eds. *Theological Dictionary of the New Testament.* Grand Rapids, MI: Eerdmans Publishing Company, 1968.

- Kohlberg, L. *The Meaning and Measurement of Moral Development.* Worcester, MA: Clark University Press, 1981.

- Ladd, George Eldon. *The Pattern of New Testament Truth.* Grand Rapids, MI: Eerdmans Publishing Company, 1968.

- Nobel Lectures, *Physiology or Medicine: 1963-1970.* Amsterdam, NL: Elsevier Publishing Company, 1972.

- Sanford, J.A. *The Man Who Wrestled With God.* New York, NY: Paulist Press, 1987.

- White, E.G. *Education.* Hagerstown, MD: Review and Herald Publishing Company, 1903.

- Wilkinson, David. *The Message of Creation.* Leicester, UK: Inter-Varsity Press, 2002.

- Willard, Dallas. *The Spirit of the Disciplines.* London, UK: Hodder & Stoughton, 1988.

# ABOUT THE AUTHOR

For more information about the author,
please contact him at:

**graeme.loftus@gmail.com**

---

Another book by Graeme Loftus:

*The Sabbath and the Trinity*
ISBN: 978-075-689-2

Additional copies of this book and other book
titles from DESTINY IMAGE™ EUROPE
are available at your local bookstore.

We are adding new titles every month!

To view our complete catalog online, visit us at:
**www.eurodestinyimage.com**

Send a request for a catalog to:

**Via Acquacorrente, 6**
**65123 - Pescara - ITALY**
**Tel. +39 085 4716623 - Fax +39 085 9431270**

*"Changing the world, one book at a time."*

---

Are you an author?

Do you have a "today" God-given message?

## CONTACT US

We will be happy to review your manuscript
for the possibility of publication:

publisher@eurodestinyimage.com
http://www.eurodestinyimage.com/pages/AuthorsAppForm.htm